Australia's Natural Wonders

Australia's Natural Wonders

Vincent Serventy

CHILD & ASSOCIATES
AN ALL-AUSTRALIAN PUBLISHER

Fraser Island, Queensland (see page 62). (Gunther Deichmann)

Title page:
Geikie Gorge, about 20 kilometres northeast of Fitzroy Crossing in
the Kimberleys (see pages 149–51). (Gunther Deichmann)

Published in 1987 under licence from
Weldon Publishing, a division of
Kevin Weldon & Associates Pty Limited
by Child & Associates Publishing Pty Ltd
5 Skyline Place, Frenchs Forest, NSW,
Australia, 2086
A wholly owned Australian publishing company
Reprinted 1989

First published by Rigby Publishers 1984
Reprinted 1986

ISBN 0 86777 259 X.

Printed in Hong Kong by Everbest
Printing Co. Ltd

Contents

THE GEOLOGICAL TIME SCALE

Relative Duration of Eras

CAINOZOIC

MESOZOIC

PALEOZOIC

1,000 m.y.

2,000 m.y.

3,000 m.y.

★ FIRST FOSSILS

4,000 m.y.

PRECAMBRIAN

Era	Period	Epoch	Million years ago
CAINOZOIC	**QUATERNARY** 1-2 million years	**RECENT** — about 10,000 years **PLEISTOCENE** — 1-2 million years	‹ 2
	TERTIARY about 63 million years	**PLIOCENE** about 3 m.y.	c. 5
		MIOCENE about 19 m.y.	c. 23
		OLIGOCENE about 15 m.y.	c. 38
		EOCENE about 16 m.y.	c. 54
		PALEOCENE about 11 m.y.	c. 65
MESOZOIC	**CRETACEOUS** about 75 m.y.		c. 140
	JURASSIC about 60 m.y.		c. 200
	TRIASSIC about 25 m.y.		c. 225
PALEOZOIC	**PERMIAN** about 55 m.y.		c. 280
	CARBONIFEROUS about 60 m.y.		c. 360
	DEVONIAN about 40 m.y.		c. 400
	SILURIAN about 40 m.y.		c. 440
	ORDOVICIAN about 60 m.y.		c. 500
	CAMBRIAN about 70 m.y.		c. 570
	PRECAMBRIAN		

Oldest known earth rocks — about 3,900 m.y.

Formation of the earth — more than 4,500 million years ago

© 1983

J. M. Scrymgour (S.A. Museum)

Introduction

THE AUSTRALIAN LANDSCAPE

What an extraordinary land this is! Try to recall any other developed country where an incredibly beautiful area could remain almost unknown within a few hundred kilometres of a major town.

Until a few years ago the Bungle Bungle, a triangle of mountains, valleys and plains near Kununurra, invaded by white cattlemen in 1908 then abandoned a few years later, was not mentioned in the tourist literature or even explored by naturalists. People flying to southern cattle stations sometimes gazed down at the remarkable collection of strangely marked cliffs, cupolas and chasms, and wondered.

Some years ago a journalist wrote about the area and since then a few more people have explored the Bungle Bungle, claiming it as the most beautiful landscape in Australia.

Again, although many Australians knew that southwest Tasmania was a wilderness of great beauty, who would have thought twenty years ago that a misty blue gorge with tumbling brown waters would become a familiar sight on television screens around the nation?

Or thought that, to save this fragile beauty a massive political struggle would take place—a battle which would help defeat a government and bring a new concept to the legal powers of the federation?

Many of the first settlers perceived a dull landscape and the myth they created has persisted, so that even some who live in Australia now do not deny it has a certain monotony when compared with Europe and other places of the northern hemisphere.

Monotony? When we have in the Great Barrier Reef the most beautiful and varied underwater wonderland in the world, a marine shoreline along our eastern and southern coasts the equal of any, and an arid west and centre of such magnificent colour that there could be no-one immune to its savage splendour.

Australia has been clothed with a bewildering number of plants: massive forest trees, their height equalled only by the giant redwoods of the west coast of America; heathlands with a variety of flowers equalled only by those in the southern tip of Africa; and rainforests whose rich number of species compare with those of more tropical lands.

So how then did this myth of monotony arise and later become reinforced? I think because Europeans saw the natural landscape of Australia in terms of their man-made countryside and the two cannot justly be compared.

Imagine Europe with all its churches, houses, cities, roads, bridges, temples, pyramids and the like, removed. Think of a trip through southern England where instead of London, Winchester and Bristol you see only rolling downs covered with forest and heather. Try to visualise the countryside as the ancient Britons saw it when they pushed their way through forests of oak, and further to the north, the dull green oceans of pine.

Compare the New Forest of England with the karri country of the southwest and the mountain ash of southeast Australia! Compare the stormy coasts of Europe with the seascapes of the Roaring Forties of southern Australia. Which have the greatest grandeur?

The same picture could be recreated for everywhere in the northern world. Only in the few national parks can you glimpse the land as it once was. Our many habitats lack nothing in variety. Because of our position in the world's latitudes we do not possess the abundant herring and other fisheries of the north Atlantic Ocean, yet we have as many species as that ocean holds in one small section of the Great Barrier Reef.

The few species of trees that dominate the forests of Europe are overshadowed by the hundreds of species that grow in any forest of Australia.

There is also no question that the world of man's making is an interesting one. We should compare Europe with Australia's man-changed landscapes. With Sydney Harbour, where the beauty of water and cliffs is enhanced by the architectural glory of the Opera House, or with the farming country of the Derwent Valley in Tasmania and around Scone in New South Wales.

All Australia lacks are the thousands of years of change and the buildings created by long-gone civilisations. We can already see how interest in our man-made heritage is growing in Australia and with

Left and over page:
Rainforest on Central Station, Fraser Island, Qld.

The Bungle Bungle is a magnificent landscape of mountain and plain almost unknown a few years ago. Its potential as a national park is being investigated.

time and good planning our man-made landscapes will one day compare with those of Europe.

The land we describe in this book is the world where man is not in control, where nature still manages the wild. If that American sage Henry David Thoreau was right when he said that in wildness is the preservation of the world, we are the lucky country.

Thoreau said, 'We need the tonic of wildness—to wade sometimes in marshes where the bittern and the meadow-hen lurk, and hear the booming of the snipe... At the same time that we are earnest to explore all things and learn all things, we require that all things be mysterious and unexplorable, that land and sea be infinitely wild, unsurveyed, and unfathomed by us because unfathomable. We can never have enough of nature'.

This book should bring you a taste of the Australian wildness and, we hope, stimulate you to experience it at first hand. You may not wish to raft down the Franklin, but you can explore in some comfort most of the places described here.

THE SHAPING OF AUSTRALIA

How the Australian landscape was shaped is a complex story and many of the details have yet to be unravelled. We do know that ours has been a restless earth since its formation some four and a half billion years ago, and it is that vast period of time that helps explain many of the features we see today. The old saying 'constant dripping wears away the hardest stone', when transmuted from a few years to millions of years, gives the major clue as to how the land was shaped.

To the work of water must be added the effects of changing temperature, ice expanding as it freezes, the bombardment of wind as it tosses sand grains at rocks, and the mighty power of waves as they batter sea cliffs, not only with sand grains but also with heavy boulders.

The very earth itself is in a state of flux. Continents drift on vast plates, are drawn deep into earth to emerge aeons later. Lands tilt and dip below the sea to rise again carrying a burden of fossil shells and other marine creatures that are exposed high on mountaintops.

Ice ages lock up vast amounts of water recycled from the oceans as frozen sheets and expose huge expanses of continental shelf. As the ice melts the sea floods back again and Australia is isolated from Tasmania and New Guinea, to which it was formerly joined.

Volcanoes, earthquakes, changing climates that cause deserts to replace rainforests, the action of plants in protecting the thin skin of soil, and the grazing of animals that exposes it, the forces of erosion—all these are part of the drama of creating the landscape we see today.

It is an enthralling story and we tell something of it when describing the various landforms that are the natural wonders of Australia.

Victoria

THE VOLCANIC REGIONS

Victoria has had two great periods during its fairly recent history when volcanoes dominated the region. The Older Volcanics, as they are called, are abundant in eastern Gippsland and belong to the geological era called the Lower Tertiary. The rocks now seen on the surface are only eroded remnants, although their depths reach about 300 metres.

The Newer Volcanics average about half this depth but are much more recent, ranging from 4·5 million years ago to times so near the present that their deposits appear quite fresh. Those at Tower Hill are believed to have been formed in an eruption as recent as between 6–7,000 years ago.

The deposits from this series of eruptions stretch from near Melbourne westward to Portland and cover an area of 15,000 square kilometres. The volcanoes which formed the Mount Gambier complex in South Australia, and are of the same general period of underground upwellings, appear even younger. These erupted about 4,800 years ago and an ash deposit was pushed out by steam as short a time ago as 1,500 years.

Despite the size of this volcanic plain, among the largest in the world, few prominent mountains were formed from the flows of lava and eruptions of ash and other ejected material. A few volcanoes reach 200 metres in height, but most are less than 100 metres.

What they lack in height they make up in numbers. One geologist recorded 123 places where material was ejected, in an area of only 1,500 square kilometres. Another researcher found twenty-one points of outflow in an area of 50 square kilometres near Mount Holden and many of them can be seen today as small humps rising from the plain.

A number of these volcanic remnants have been used for quarries of rock, but some have been preserved as national parks or similar reserves.

Organ Pipes

The landforms produced by the Newer Volcanics are varied. Among the minor patterns which can still produce spectacular scenery are those that create columns. Such a structure develops when a liquid material hardens. It can be seen on the surface of a creek when the moist mud shrinks into hexagonal patterns on drying.

In the case of lava flows shapes of this kind develop not only on the surface as the rock cools but also throughout the lava flow. For these to become more than a surface feature the rock must cool slowly and then the column continues through the whole mass. Such columnar jointing as it is called is not common in Victoria, but the example preserved at the Organ Pipes National Park, 8 kilometres past Keilor, is a good one.

About a million years ago great masses of molten rock flowed from volcanoes near Macedon and Mount Holden, spreading over the Keilor Plains and filling valleys. At this spot the lava filled a creek bed running at right angles to the present Jackson's Creek and reached a depth of about 70 metres. Because of this thickness the cooling was slow, an ideal condition for vertical cracks to develop as the rock began to contract, while at the same time the pillars took a hexagonal shape in cross-section due to the shrinking.

Over the years a new creek line developed and the present Jackson's Creek eroded away the volcanic rocks to reveal the deep-buried columns which now line the sides of the creek valley in several places. The basalt columns look like the pipes of a large organ—hence the name.

The lava flow covered more ancient sandstone rocks containing fossils, which have been dated at 400 million years in age and add enormous interest to this 65 hectare national park.

Another smaller feature called the Rosette Rock is a number of basalt columns radiating like the spokes of a wheel. How this rock ever formed is still a puzzle.

Most of the organ pipes are six-sided, but five or seven-sided columns can be formed. Other volcanic landforms found in this reserve are tessellated pavements.

Here erosion has worn the columns to make a bed of the creek about a kilometre upstream.

MOUNT ELEPHANT

The smooth grey bulk of this dome heaving its way above the land surface resembles the back of a giant elephant pushing out of greenery.

Its steep sides are due to the variable nature of lava flows. Basalts which have less silica are often called basic lavas and are very fluid, often travelling at a speed of up to 15 kilometres an hour. Down a valley the flow may reach 60 kilometres an hour.

Acid lavas, rich in silica, are the reverse. Being sticky these move slowly. Gas often bubbles out from the material making the surface look like a froth. Pumice is a good example of a volcanic rock so filled with bubbles that it is extraordinarily light for its size.

When such rocks have a spongy surface they are called scoriaceous or scoria. On the volcanic plains of western Victoria scoria cones are common and as the material is coarse the slopes can build to inclines of 40 to 45 degrees before the material begins to slide.

Such hillocks are often called cinder cones. They are among the younger landforms, created recently by volcanic action, so erosion has had little effect and they appear almost as fresh as when they were made. Often the wall of the crater is broken on one side and lava has poured through this outlet.

Mount Elephant is the highest of such scoria cones on these western volcanic plains, but its symmetry has been partly spoiled by quarrying for bluestone metal (a term often used to describe volcanic or similar rocks used commercially).

TOWER HILL

Nature's fireworks must have caused the Aboriginal inhabitants of southeast Australia a great deal of excitement and fear during their long occupation of this continent.

Possibly between 5,500 and 6,000 years ago a violent explosion in the present Tower Hill region shot masses of rocks into the sky and caused vast flows of lava to pour across the countryside.

The explosion was of the same kind as that recorded in Roman times at Vesuvius and more recently at Krakatoa, when this island was destroyed. This western Victorian blast may have been produced by groundwater flowing through breaks in the limestone bedrock and coming into contact with molten rock. The blast from water converted from a liquid into vapour could send rock fragments hurtling into the air. Those that settled to earth as a sediment are called Tower Hill tuff.

As steam pressure dropped the structure collapsed making the deep crater of Tower Hill. This volcanic crater, 3·2 kilometres long and 2·4 kilometres wide, is regarded as the largest in Australia. Later it was filled by a number of smaller craters, twenty of them in all, which built up their own miniature landforms inside the huge mother hollow. Such a structure is called a nested caldera.

Tower Hill rises gently from the surrounding plain, the daughter craters inside its steep sides. The crater hollow became filled with water, so creating the present lake, and the smaller eruptions became islands.

The volcanic rock weathered to good soils. With the reasonable rainfall it is no surprise that in the early days of white settlement visitors spoke of a heavy undergrowth of ferns as well as thick forests.

A well-known educational writer, James Bonwick, wrote in 1857, 'A stroll among the gigantic ferns of the valley, or a ramble among the cones and craters, has peculiar attractions. But these are not comparable to the winding path at the foot of the basaltic rises close to the lake. There the graceful Fern tree waves . . . almost tropical reeds rustle in the breeze . . . leafy shrubs and trees form delightful bowers and alcoves . . .'

A few years later the work of destruction began and trees were cleared and quarries begun. Conservation pressure forced governments to take action as far back as 1866 when 600 hectares were reserved to protect the geological features. Then in 1892 came its declaration as the first Victorian National Park.

Finally in 1981 it was handed over to the Fisheries and Wildlife Service to be managed as a game reserve. A natural history centre educates visitors on the scientific interest of Tower Hill and today this landform is one of the major attractions of the district.

THE MURRAY RIVER

Of all the continents, Australia has the least annual rain or snowfall, apart from Antarctica, which is even drier. Therefore any large river was of great importance to the early explorers, both Aboriginal and European.

The course of the Murray River today runs through desert and semi-desert. When the Aboriginals settled along this mightiest of rivers is still a mystery but it was certainly 40,000 years ago, possibly earlier.

The country around the Murray would have been lusher then than it is today, and as the land dried out the waters of the Murray would have become even more important for food would always be plentiful nearby. Grey kangaroos, wallabies, possums and koalas, freshwater tortoises, fish and yabbies, freshwater mussels and witchetty grubs are still common here and tubers of sedges and bulrushes as well as other plants offered an ever-present supply of the plant food most Aboriginal groups depended on.

In recent 'digs' by archaeologists in Kow Swamp, an area fed by the Murray in flood, and the burial ground of an Aboriginal clan which lived here between 9,500 and 13,500 years ago, bones were found that show a more archaic character than those of native peoples who lived more than 26,000 years ago in the north. Although older the northern bones have a more modern form.

The people of ancient Egypt were able to withstand incursions by invaders and it is possible that those more archaic Aboriginals, through their prior occupation of this river stronghold and weight of numbers, were able to force newcomers from the north to flow around their country and leave them in possession.

The explorer, Charles Sturt, examined much of this river system and its northern tributaries and made this perceptive. comment, 'The natives look to this periodical overflow of their river, with as much anxiety as did ever or now do the Egyptians, to the overflowing of the Nile. To both they are the bountiful dispensation of a beneficent Creator, for as the sacred stream rewards the husbandman with a double harvest, so does the Murray replenish the exhausted reservoirs of the poor children of the desert with numberless fish, and resuscitates myriads of crayfish that had laid dormant underground; without which supply of food, and the flocks of wild fowl that at the same time cover the creeks and lagoons, it is more than probable, the first navigators of the Murray would not

have heard a human voice along its banks . . .'

It was always the presence of permanent water which was the basis for the survival of groups everywhere on this arid continent, but today we know that those 'poor children of the desert' lived a rich and interesting life; a nomadic existence with an involvement in both religion and art.

Sturt recorded that the rise and fall of the waters of the river were gradual, noting '. . . it receives the first additions to its waters from the eastward, in the month of July, and rises at the rate of an inch a day until December, in which month it attains a height of about seventeen feet above its lowest or winter levels. As it rises it fills in succession all its lateral creeks and lagoons, and it ultimately lays many of its flats under water'.

This happy state of affairs had occasional checks when long droughts reduced the Murray and its tributaries to chains of pools; but there was always some water.

A person might walk dryshod across the river bed one year, to find in the next that the same stream was 100 kilometres wide. It was this variation in flow that finally killed almost all the shipping industry on the Murray and the other major rivers. A paddlesteamer which went to Bourke in the last century had to wait there for three years until flood waters came once more and released it.

Modern storage dams changed this natural system and also produced changes in the wildlife that depend on these waters—many of the native fish can no longer breed because of lack of water. The lower summer levels today are due to the holding back of winter and spring floods in the Hume Dam and other

Lake Hattah National Park near Mildura is a haven for wildlife.

storages, for release in summer for irrigation.

The word 'river' comes from a Latin term meaning a divider and much of the Murray marks the boundary between the states of Victoria and New South Wales. How did the Murray develop into the giant river it is today? The catchment for the Murray covers one-seventh of Australia, an area of more than one million square kilometres. It has a length of 2,600 kilometres and an even longer tributary in the Darling with 2,740 kilometres. The Goulburn, 560 kilometres long and the Murrumbidgee, 1,575 kilometres long, are the other two major tributaries.

In spite of these lengthy tributaries the Murray still provides a quarter of the total runoff. This is because the rainfall in the catchment area of the Australian Alps is heavy and reliable, although this section upstream of Albury totals less than a fifth of the intake areas.

Unfortunately the impressive catchments do not provide impressive quantities of water, except in very occasional years. Accurate measurements have been taken since 1909 and during 1914, 1915, 1923 and 1946 the river dwindled to no more than a string of waterholes with no flow.

Because of the low slope of many of the beds in this river system, rain which falls in the mountains does not reach the sea for two months. High evaporation also means that a great deal of water is lost on the way.

The geological history of the Murray has been at least partly unravelled. More than 50 million years ago sea covered much of Australia and the first Murray system developed when the land was uplifted above the waters. There came another smaller invasion of the sea that reached as far inland as Deniliquin. The results of this incursion are described in the section dealing with the Murray Gorges and their fossil beds in South Australia.

Despite all these changes the Murray kept pouring west and south to the sea, although in that time the Darling had a separate outlet to the ocean. Then came the tilting of the South Australian landscape that produced Mount Lofty and the Flinders Ranges. This turned the river south to find a new exit to the sea.

The river rushes headlong down slopes from its beginning in the Indi River. Other streams such as the Ovens, the King and the Kiewa add their quota and the boisterous stream slowly subsides to a more gently flowing one when it reaches the plain country and the arid regions of the mallee.

During this long period the Murray wandered lazily across the countryside changing its course often and leaving behind oxbow lakes. Two particular areas have become famous. One is the uplift which took place across the river path. Geologists call this area the Cadell Tilt

Block and it broke the Murray into two streams: one flows south past Barmah while the other runs near Deniliquin.

The country between these two arms of the river floods in good years, making about 4,500 hectares of lakes, swamps and forests. The Barmah State Forest is a wilderness of river redgums growing on the flood plains. It is famous for its timber production and equally famous for its wildlife. It was important to the Aboriginals and later to the squatters as a grazing area for stock. Today the blossoms of the yellow and black box also growing in this section of the river plain produce high-quality honey.

South of Mildura is another of the many diversions of the Murray—the Hattah Lakes system with some twenty lakes. Many of them are important wildlife sanctuaries. In most years the stretches of water are separate pools, gradually drying out. At each new flooding of the Murray River water pours along these dried-out watercourses, filling lake after lake to the brim and completing a great semi-circle before returning to the parent stream.

Some 48,000 hectares of the lake system is preserved as the Murray-Kulkyne National Park that stretches from the Calder Highway to the Murray River and the fascinating wildlife of the mallee forests is added to that of the billabongs, lakes and riversides.

These are only two of the Murray's side excursions, examples of the diversity which has made this stream and its surrounds one of the great recreational areas of three states.

WILSONS PROMONTORY

When Bass and Flinders completed their incredibly daring and skillful explorations in Bass Strait they asked that this landmark be named in honour of their London friend, Thomas Wilson.

George Bass brought the promontory to the notice of white settlers with a succinct description of its major landforms, 'Its firmness and vast durability make it well worthy of being, what there is great reason to believe it is, the boundary point of a large strait and a cornerstone of this great island, New Holland. It is joined to the mainland by a low neck of sand, which is nearly divided by a lagoon that runs in on the west side of it, and by a large shoal inlet, on the east'.

Granite is the rock which produces so much of the scenery of this popular reserve. The section that outcrops to such effect in the 'Prom' is part of a 500 kilometre long belt, 50 kilometres wide, which reaches as far south as northeastern Tasmania. This vast mass was formed some 400 million years ago deep in the earth where the rocks, at 800 degrees Celsius, are molten.

As the materials move upwards before they cool and become solid they may pick

up sections of other rocks, including sediments. Sometimes these foreign bits can be seen as darker patches in the generally grey granite and geologists call them 'xenoliths'. This Latin term literally means 'foreign stones'.

It is commonly believed that granites are fairly uniform rocks of little interest to scientists, but investigations have shown that this is not true. During the change from molten to solid rock different structures develop, and it has recently been discovered that there are two main granite masses. Some showed patterns rather similar to sediments as they developed into sheets of material between 10 and 100 metres thick.

Over the hundreds of millions of years since its formation, when thousands of metres of rock above the granites were removed by erosion, stresses in the great granite mass produced, not only major faults, but also the joints common in most rocks.

Such weaknesses, and changing sea levels as well, helped produce the landforms we see today. Fault lines are places where rivers can cut more easily,

Above:
Wilsons Promontory is connected to the mainland by the lowlying Yanakie Isthmus, seen in the distance from Corner Inlet.

Left:
Valleys such as Lilly Pilly Gully are good examples of streams etched into old fault lines.

and valleys such as Lilly Pilly Gully and the upper parts of Tidal River are good examples of streams etched into old fault lines.

The joints running at right angles to each other break up solid sections into blocks which become rounded by weathering into the tors and other smooth shapes that are a feature of so much of this national park.

Fingers of more resistant rock, left after the sea eroded along joint lines, enclose sandy beaches that delight summer visitors.

On this foundation of rocks changing climates caused other landforms. The two kinds of sand dunes along the margins of the Prom often puzzle visitors. The dunes to the east are of white sands rich in silica with little lime, while to the west are yellow sands, over one-third lime, the rest being silica.

The solution to this mystery is believed to be that when Wilsons Promontory was an island about 100,000 years ago the white sand drifted across and down the west coast. Then came the new ice ages when the sea levels dropped and the island was joined to Victoria and Tasmania. The white silica sands collected on the east side while the prevailing winds from the west brought the lime-rich yellow sands, moving some of them inland to form 100 metre thick dunes.

As the ice melted the seas returned and Bass Strait was reformed some 11,000 years ago, but the Prom did not become an island once more. It remained firmly tied to the mainland by the sandy isthmus of the Yanakie Peninsula.

One beach has become famous as a musical landform. The Victorian naturalists, E. R. Thomas and J. M. Lones, studied the material of Squeaky Beach and found that when sand grains are of uniform size, a moving foot causes small masses of the grains to strike each other and give off a particular note. 'Singing sands' are found not only along much of our coastlines, but also in other parts of the world, including deserts.

In other low-lying areas, sand dunes blocked river and creek flow to create swamps. The Aboriginals must have found the region a good hunting and

gathering ground, but due to the changing sea levels over the last 100,000 years the middens they accumulated around important campsites are now buried under the sea. Future archaeologists may have to become underwater explorers to study them.

There are a few old campsites near the northern end of the park that now lie about half a kilometre inland. Radioactive carbon datings have measured them as being 6,500 years old. It is interesting to note that about 1,000 years ago the local Aboriginal diet changed from the molluscs gathered on rocky shores to different species which flourish on sandy beaches; this piece of research-finding is evidence of a fresh influx of sand covering the rocky reefs.

The Prom was reserved as a National Park in 1909 and was steadily increased to its present area of 49,000 hectares, making it one of the largest in Victoria.

There are 700 species of plants in Wilsons Promontory and so great is the interest in them that a Victorian naturalist, J. Ros Garnet, published a book dealing solely with the flowers of the park. Mammals in the Prom include grey kangaroos, which are the largest marsupials found there, plus pigmy possums which are at the lower end of the size scale. Before the declaration of the park many wallaby and koala skins were shipped out of the area, but today with strict protection koalas and other mammals are increasing.

The Prom has always been a birdwatcher's paradise and over 60 per cent of Victoria's avifauna has been recorded here. The long history of protection has meant that camps such as the one at Tidal River are haunts of birds which are remarkably tame. Even those with little natural history knowledge can enjoy intimate glimpses into the life of the birds of this reserve.

The late Roy Cooper was one of the keenest of the ornithologists and he and his friends put thousands of man-hours into a study of the birdlife. Mr Cooper

pointed out the importance of the saw banksia to the honey-eating birds of the park and urged that more of these plants should be planted to replace those destroyed earlier.

The National Park management is not only concerned with keeping the wildlife quality of the reserve, but also with developing walking tracks so that the flood of visitors each year will not destroy the fragile soils and the plants they contain.

One favoured walking track of 44 kilometres runs right round The Prom and is recommended as a three-day trip. Detailed maps provide information on distances, camping areas and watering points, as well as places where the scenic grandeur is best revealed.

There are also nature trails. The one at Lilly Pilly Gully has an educational booklet which describes the landforms of the Prom and the associated wildlife, and even informs the visitor that although the recommended time for the trail is three hours, it can be covered by 6,961 average-sized paces!

The reserve includes thirteen offshore islands that are sanctuaries for sea birds of many species. This most southerly point of the mainland with its peaks rearing 600 metres above the sea will always remain a prime favourite with Victorians.

THE GRAND CANYON OF THE GRAMPIANS

Much of the Grampians is forest reserve managed for multiple use or crown land, and conservationists have been trying to get some sections managed as a national park.

This western end of the Great Dividing Range is a major water catchment area, a source of timber; farmland; and above all a great recreational magnet for the western districts.

The rocks of the Grampians are mainly folded sandstones that run north to south for 100 kilometres, and east and west for 50 kilometres. Because of the gentle slope of the sediments to the east, erosion has carved out an escarpment steeper to the east than the west and it was this that led explorer Thomas Mitchell to name the area after the Grampians in Scotland. Geologists call this kind of landform a cuesta.

Long before the white explorers reached here the Aboriginals found it good country. The evidence of their long occupation can be seen in old campsites marked by middens and rock paintings. There are also a few 'canoe trees', where scars on the trunk show where some long-ago Aboriginal found a suitable piece of material to make a frail boat to use on the local rivers and lakes.

Left:
The dramatic beauty of the Wilsons Promontory coastline is shown particularly well in this photograph of Whisky Beach.

Right:
Halls Gap from Boroka Lookout, The Grampians.

The Grampians lie at the western end of the Great Dividing Range. All year round walks offer scenic grandeur, while in the springtime the wildflowers are a major attraction.

Far right:
McKenzie Falls, The Grampians.

Over (pp. 10–11):
The Razorback Ridge running to Mt Feathertop from the Hotham Heights in the Bogong National Park.

The Grand Canyon is part of a two-hour walk from the Turntable to the Pinnacle. It is a miniature gorge similar to many of the canyons in Australia where sandstone beds have been broken by vertical joints. Along these joints a valley with steep walls has gradually been eroded. The residual rocks that give variety to the gorge have also been shaped by erosion.

In this canyon, as with so much of the Grampians, the grandeur of the landforms is enhanced by the diversity of the wildlife and the abundant spring wildflowers. A booklet devoted entirely to the Grampians' plants has also been published.

The habitats here vary from wet and dry forests to heath and savannah woodland, and in these hundreds of thousands of hectares a great variety of plants feed and shelter a great variety of animals. There are more than 200 kinds of birds, and marsupials are abundant in numbers and species.

Koalas feed in the manna gums. They were increased in 1957 by a large number taken from French Island. This kind of release is a practical form of conservation which should be used with other rare animals.

You can visit the Grampians for the craggy rocks of places such as the Grand Canyon, for its wildlife, for its Aboriginal art, for the bushwalking or for any combination of these—there are attractions for all.

BOGONG HIGH PLAINS

'As early as October, as soon as the snow had melted on the lower ranges, small parties of natives would start during fine weather for some of the frostriven rocks and procure "Bugongs" for food. A great gathering usually took place about Christmas on the highest ranges, when sometimes from 500 to 700 aborigines belonging to different friendly tribes would assemble almost solely for the purpose of feasting upon roasted moths. Sometimes these natives had to come great distances to enjoy this food, which was not only much appreciated by them but must have been very nutritious, because their condition was generally improved by it and when they returned from the mountains their skins looked glossy and most of them were quite fat.'

The above piece was written by naturalist Richard Helms after he visited the high country in 1889. He describes a pattern of food gathering followed for thousands of years. In *The Moth Hunters* the archaeologist, Dr Josephine Flood, gives fascinating details of this story of the moths and the men who sought them.

The bogong, or bugong moth as it is sometimes called, develops from a caterpillar that feeds on the grasses of lowland areas before changing to the winged form. It then flies to the high country in southeast Australia and collects in large numbers in caves in the hills above 1,370 metres.

An account from the Bogong High Plains in the mid-1880s shows that some natives also liked to feast on the grubs, 'The caterpillars of it are exceedingly abundant, and formed, half-roasted, at certain seasons, a favourite food of the Australian natives. The natives called these caterpillars "Bogong", which name was afterwards applied to the habitat of the Bogong'.

Soon after the discovery of the high grass-covered country, the first white settlers moved their livestock to the lush pastures every summer. By early autumn the stock would be moved down again in good condition. To 'improve' the quality of the grasslands the graziers practised an Aboriginal technique called firestick farming—using fire to improve both the palatability and the value of the plants.

A mystique of the mountain men—as tough as the horses they rode and the country they rode over—developed down the years. Naturalists, while not ignoring the romance of these myths, began to worry about what was happening to the high country itself.

Fortunately the Bogong High Plains resisted all such burning by graziers, although they were apparently swept out by the disastrous fires of January 1939.

In 1945 fenced and unfenced experimental plots were established to study the effect of the summer grazing. This work was continued until 1977, but long before it was completed it became obvious that grazing was damaging the plains as well as increasing soil erosion, and the pattern was the same throughout the high country of southeast Australia. Cattle grazing was reduced in 1946 on the Bogong High Plains as well as in many other areas.

Today some of the more valuable natural history and scenic regions have been reserved as national parks, although Victorian conservationists are still working for a huge Alpine National Park similar to the Kosciusko National Park in New South Wales.

A new 400 kilometre long alpine walking track from Mount Erica in Victoria to Tom Groggin in New South Wales, passes through the rugged high country of the area and across the Bogong High Plains.

How these high plains were originally formed has been described in the section on Kosciusko. The Bogong is the largest area of treeless high country in the alpine region, a 'sea of grass' surrounded by peaks.

From Mount Feathertop a visitor can see the plains, the bluff strength of Mount Bogong and the backdrop of the Kosciusko Main Range, as well as the tree-filled valleys of this dissected landscape.

The highlands are the important catchment for Victoria, with a water yield about five times as high as that from a similar area below 1,000 metres. Increasingly they are becoming a major recreation area for interstate visitors as well as for Victorians.

PORT CAMPBELL NATIONAL PARK

Few landforms of Australia are more photographed than this impressive mingling of land, sea and sky along a 30-kilometre stretch of the Victorian coastline.

This area of offshore stacks, rugged cliffs and small islands is described by geologists as a high-energy coast. Here the full force of the waves driven by the Roaring Forties are felt as they move in a great and unbroken sweep around the southern oceans.

Figures show the tremendous power of the sea as a battering ram. In one European storm the windows in a lighthouse were broken when the waves, 65 metres below, lifted rocks broken away from the shoreline to this great height.

In Sherbon Hills' book *Physiography of Victoria* the details are recorded of a rock 3 tonnes in weight being thrown over a 7 metre high wall. A famous example from Sydney Heads is of a 250 tonne piece of sandstone being shifted from the edge of the reef to its present position in a great storm in 1912. The rock is now used as the base of a bronze mermaid statue.

A violent storm can cause an impact pressure of 30 tonnes per square metre—an impressive blow which wears away the most solid of rocks. At Port Campbell this power is enhanced by the fact that the sedimentary beds of Miocene limestones are horizontal and the waters

Top right and right:
Winter in Bogong National Park shows alpine ash with a powdering of snow. Many eucalypt species have evolved to handle a variety of climatic extremes.

Top and above:
The Island Archway at Port Campbell.

Left:
Port Campbell National Park is one of the most visited and admired of all Australian landforms. Here in the horizontally bedded limestones of the coast, storm waves have carved a fascinating series of stacks, bridges, headlands and arches.

Over (pp. 14–15):
Loch Ard Gorge at Port Campbell.

can work along the lines of weakness of the beds, as well as along the joints which fracture it.

Some storms have bevelled ledges up to 60 metres above the sea on this coastline. A visible example of how the land is retreating due to sea erosion is shown by Elephant Rock, a landform that lost its trunk as the sea ate away at its base.

If blows come from both sides to a headland under wave attack then caves are cut into the rock. Finally they join to form a natural arch similar to London Bridge, Island Archway and Marble Arch in the Port Campbell National Park. Eventually the arch breaks, leaving an island or stack.

The best-known stacks are the Twelve Apostles which rise 100 metres above the sea. With continuing erosion the stacks dwindle and disappear under the waves. They can be seen as shallow platforms as waves ebb, revealing the lighter-coloured area beneath.

The Blowhole, a 400 metre long passage which channels storm waters that climax in a terrifying spectacle, is another structure cut by the sea. The end of the blowhole has a depth of about 15 metres and a diameter of nearly 40 metres.

The national park publications call this area the graveyard of ships, as five have been destroyed along the coastline. The most tragic loss was when the three-

The Twelve Apostles, a line of stacks isolated from the mainland by the eroding power of the waves.

masted iron clipper *Loch Ard* was wrecked and fifty people lost their lives in 1878. The story of this disaster is told on a plaque at the top of the gorge.

This 750-hectare park is mainly visited for its striking views of cliffs and offshore islands, and is also home for the nesting Tasmanian muttonbird or short-tailed shearwater as well as the fairy penguin.

The park also contains an interesting variety of dune and clifftop plants. A national parks study identified 362 different kinds of plants, ranging from the delicate beauty of a host of orchids, including spiders, fairies and greenhoods, to many grasses and the colourful noonflowers that are at home in the harsh environment.

THE AUSTRALIAN ALPS

*'He hails from Snowy River, up by
   Kosciusko's side,
Where the hills are twice as steep and
   twice as rough;
Where a horse's hoofs strike firelight from
   the flint stones every stride . . .'*

The Man from Snowy River by Banjo Paterson is enshrined in the memory of every Australian. Many of us learnt this stirring saga of the mountain men by heart, and at the same time we absorbed some knowledge of the landforms of the Australian Alps—that they are steep, rocky and the home of rivers.

The outside world tends to think of Australia as hot, dry and mainly desert. This is true of much of the country, but we also have a diversity of habitats equalling those of most other continents. Winter snowfields are found in the southeast corner of the mainland and in Tasmania.

The Australian Alps straddle Victoria, New South Wales and the Australian Capital Territory and all three States have declared major national parks and similar reserves to protect this unique environment. Not forgetting the significance of its beauty and scientific value the area is also important for our recreation, our water resources and our power generation.

Dr A. B. Costin is a name to conjure with in the study of the alpine areas. A botanist, he has worked for more than 30 years in the high country, and in association with his fellow scientists has produced a classic work called *Kosciusko Alpine Flora*, as well as an entire section on the Australian Alps in *The Heritage of Australia*. This conservation 'Domesday Book', the only one of its kind in the world, lists not only our treasures in the form of the natural environment but also the outstanding achievements in our built environment.

The extent of the alpine environment is a matter of judgement. The higher places, where no trees grow, and also areas 500 metres below this where snow cover is fairly constant in winter, are usually described as 'snow country'. Tasmania has some 6,500 square kilometres of snow country and the mainland 5,200 square kilometres. Together they total about 0·15 per cent of Australia.

Dr Costin lists only 250 square kilometres as being truly alpine and 100 square kilometres of this is in the Primitive Area of the New South Wales Kosciusko National Park—an area given absolute protection for its great scientific interest.

The Alps themselves are a very large landform. The foothills are within 50 kilometres of Melbourne and the ranges run 500 kilometres northeast to the Brindabella Ranges in the Australian Capital Territory and the Snowy Mountains in New South Wales, with an average width of 50 kilometres. New South Wales has the highest point in Australia, which is Mount Kosciusko at 2,228 metres.

It would be impossible to discuss here the rocks of this vast region in any detail. Briefly, a great sea that covered much of eastern Australia some 450 million years ago provided the basin in which a variety of sediments were deposited. Slowly they were changed to the quartzites, slates, schists, and other rocks of the present day by uplift, heat and pressure.

Some 400 million years ago there was an invasion of granites whose outcrops are such a feature of Kosciusko as well as Mount Buffalo. Pushed high above the sea, the ranges of those far-off times were then reduced by erosion to a huge plain, the more resistant rocks remaining as peaks. Some 60 million years ago great earth movements began and continued until recently in geological terms, possibly only a million years ago.

When the earth shifts on such a massive scale old lines of weakness, as well as new fractures, produce faults where rivers and other erosive forces often cut deep. A map, or a view of the Alps from the air, will show a number of straight and parallel streams—the Upper Snowy, Crackenback and Guthega are good examples.

The warmer, moister climates of the Tertiary gave way during the Pleistocene Ice Ages to chilly conditions. It was then, as glaciers covered much of the alpine area, that an array of the landforms associated with ice sheets were created. Even where there were no ice sheets the soil and underlying rock were affected by the breaking power of freezing water on the surface.

Water expands instead of shrinking when it solidifies and if it penetrates a crack in a rock, the chill of winter changing the liquid to ice produces an explosive force that can shatter rocks.

Such factors combined resulted in pavements polished by ice sheets, erratics, boulders carried along by or on a glacier and then dumped far from their place of origin, and moraines, which are even larger masses of rock left when the glaciers melted.

High up on the peaks the work of snow and ice plucked out hollows in cliffs called cirques. Cirques, and basins dammed by moraines, made many of the lakes in the high country when the end of the last Ice Age about 10,000 years ago heralded a return to warmer conditions, and produced the Alps we know today.

Broadly speaking, in New South Wales the Alps are a plateau with gentle slopes and thick soil covering. The Victorian Alps, while having similar plateaux, are much more deeply eroded by rivers and have a more rugged aspect. The high points are well known to bushwalkers and skiing enthusiasts; Mount Feathertop, Buller and Bogong being among the most favourite spots.

Nature has clothed this variety of landforms and associated soils with an equal variety of plantlife, from lowly mosses to giant trees. Dr Costin has classified it into four major areas. The alpine, the most exciting places to most visitors, are those above 1,800 metres where no trees grow. In summer, blossoms of a wealth excelled only in southwestern Australia in spring flourish here, and great sweeps of the landscape disappear under the white of snow daisies or the gold of billy buttons.

The high country in summer is enthralling. One can see snowdrifts in sheltered hollows and the blue of mountain lakes amid the banks of flowers.

At lower levels on the slopes waves of snow gums advance until they are halted by the killing barrier of a belt of chilled air where the mean summer temperature falls below 10 degrees Celsius. The full glory of the many-coloured bark of the snow gum is revealed only when it is wet with rain or rubbed with snow. Then it glows in shades from white through yellow to deep red.

As one travels down the slopes trees appear. Gradually they increase in height until in the lowlands giants such as the alpine ash and other eucalypts dominate the scene.

Over 1,000 kinds of ferns and flowering plants have been recorded from this area, 10 per cent of them growing only in the alpine regions.

To the stunning beauty of the plants in the snow country is added the interest of the wildlife. I will never forget one autumn day when an early fall of snow caught many birds high in the mountains. Normally they retreat to lower levels at the first breath of winter. Crimson rosellas, pausing for a moment to glean some seeds on one small patch of clear ground, were surrounded by freshly fallen snow. Their green and crimson against the clear white was an unforgettable sight.

Gang-gang cockatoos lingered overhead in a snow gum feeding on the seeds of the tree tops. Towards dusk an occasional common wombat having trouble moving through the snow drifts could be seen searching for plant food.

It is fortunate that much of the Australian Alps has been preserved as national parks. Kosciusko with some 625,000 hectares is the largest park in New South Wales, Gudgenby Nature Reserve of 52,000 hectares is centred in the Australian Capital Territory and Victoria has a string of parks, the best known of them being Wonnongatta-Moroka with 104,000 hectares, Bogong with 79,000 hectares, Baw Baw with 13,000 hectares and Mount Buffalo with 11,000 hectares.

International standing was given to Kosciusko National Park when in 1978 it was recognised as a Biosphere Reserve, a classification developed in 1970 by three international agencies, UNESCO, UNEP and IUCN. Such reserves are defined as areas of natural and man-modified land that provide opportunities for both national and international research into environmental problems.

There is no doubt that some time in the future the Australian Alps will be nominated by the three State Governments and the Australian Government for inclusion in the World Heritage List.

New South Wales

SYDNEY HARBOUR

'I know that the task would be hopeless were I to attempt to make others understand the beauty of Sydney Harbour. I can say that it is lovely, but I cannot paint its loveliness. The sea runs up in various bays or coves, indenting the land all around the city, so as to give a thousand different aspects of the water—and not of water, broad unbroken, and unrelieved but of water always with jutting corners of land beyond it, and then again of water and then again of land . . .

Sydney is one of the places, which, when a man leaves it knowing that he will never return, he cannot leave without a pang and a tear. Such is its loveliness.'

Surely no city has ever had a more eloquent testimonial than this one by English writer Anthony Trollope in 1873.

A happening some 10,000 years ago created this juxtaposition of sea and land, for Sydney Harbour is an old river valley drowned by a rising sea. This landform, called a ria, is the same kind of meeting of earth and water which created the overwhelming beauty of the coastlines of southwest Tasmania and the Kimberleys in Western Australia.

Trollope was not the first to express his pleasure with Sydney Harbour. Captain Arthur Phillip, in search of a better harbour for a new settlement, decided to look at the 2 kilometre entrance Captain Cook had ignored, apart from calling it Port Jackson in honour of the-then Secretary of the Admiralty in England.

Sailing between the 100 metre high cliffs which flank the entrance like the towers of a castle, Phillip found himself in a shelter which he described exultantly, 'We got into Port Jackson early in the afternoon and had the satisfaction of finding the finest harbour in the world.'

Certainly it is immense. Defining Sydney Harbour as all the tidal water, it measures 55 square kilometres or 5,504 hectares, with a total distance inland of 21 kilometres. If the distance along the foreshores is measured, this increases to 240 kilometres.

As it is a drowned river valley its waters are deep, and at least half of the harbour has more than 9 metres of water at low tide. The heads themselves have 24 metres of water, and near Blue's Point the water plunges to 47 metres, the greatest depth in the 'finest harbour in the world'.

There are two main channels for shipping; one continues on past Cockatoo Island where it splits, one arm continuing a short distance up the Lane Cove River and the other running along the Parramatta River where it finally reaches the flat country of the Cumberland Plain.

The high cliffs fronting the water near the harbour mouth are Hawkesbury Sandstone, rocks originally laid down as sands in a lake in what geologists call the Sydney Basin. This was a huge depression running from near Bateman's Bay in the south, northward to Port Stephens and inland to Jenolan and Lithgow.

The rocks of this vast basin were also laid down over much of eastern New South Wales and their full extent is not yet certain. They all belong to the Permian and Triassic periods, have a total thickness of more than 4,000 metres and include coal seams. The 300 metres of the Hawkesbury Sandstone at the heads was probably deposited in a freshwater delta.

The mighty dinosaurs that trod the earth for at least 150 million years had their beginnings in this Triassic period and although their fossils have not yet been found in this area, they would have wandered along the shores of this 'Sydney Basin' lake.

Then came the uplifting of the whole area and the Parramatta River began its slow work of erosion until it was drowned by the rising sea level as icecaps around the world melted at the close of the last ice age.

Because the present drainage basins of the Parramatta and Lane Cove Rivers are so small, there is very little silt in the harbour. Nearer the sea there is evidence, from their height and from the sandy links with the rest of the land, that North and South Heads were once islands, to be finally tied to the land by sandbars, just as Barrenjoey is linked to Palm Beach.

The harbour is a treasure house for the naturalist. The deep waters shelter at least 400 kinds of fish, as well as corals, sea urchins, and a host of other marine creatures, and along the bushland foreshores reptiles, birds and mammals, such as the brushtail possum, add interest.

The natural beauty of the harbour, as well as the good fortune which kept some of the foreshore as natural bushland, led to conservationists suggesting that all the natural sections be dedicated as a Sydney Harbour National Park. Their efforts bore fruit when the first sections were declared in 1975. Since then more sections have been added, although there is still a long way to go before the conservation position can be considered satisfactory.

Yet it is a beginning, and means that in 100 years' time other travellers will still be able to echo Trollope's words, of leaving Sydney Harbour with reluctance, and the residents will still be refreshed every day by its loveliness.

LAKE GEORGE—THE DISAPPEARING LAKE

Many a local lake is thought 'bottomless' and lakes that suddenly appear, or worse, disappear, are found in most states. Midway between Goulburn and Canberra is a well-known disappearing lake—Lake George.

The Aboriginals had a legend that the water went into great holes in the ground. The white settlers, having seen it dry four times since the early days, decided to regard it as mysterious.

Yet in our dry land, lakes which form, then vanish, are common. There is no mystery—the water which originally came from the sky in the form of rain goes back into the sky in the form of water vapour. Lake Eyre is a classic example of an area large enough to be thought of as an inland sea when full, yet it has filled only twice in white memory.

Lake George is a hollow with no creek outlets situated in country which only has an annual rainfall of about 650 millimetres. In typical Australian fashion this rain can be erratic and both floods and droughts are common. In a series of wet years the lake fills; in a series of drought years it empties once more.

When full it plays an important part in the local scene, especially for recreation; and in earlier days a paddle steamer carted wool across it, bullock teams taking over when the lake was dry. When the waters went the lake bottom was fenced and used for grazing.

When full its 20,000 hectares of surface can become dangerous in high winds and there have been yachting tragedies. Fishermen found it a delight and on good weekends stood shoulder to shoulder to reap the harvest of redfins which averaged a kilogram in weight. Two hundred fish an hour was a common catch for those who used boats.

Yet there were no fish in the lake when the white settlers arrived. The first introduction was Murray Cod. These flourished and as the waters receded farmers came to pitchfork the dead fish into drays to use as manure. At the next filling brown and rainbow trout were introduced and later redfin; Prussian carp came in without any recorded assistance. It was the later introductions, such as trout and redfin, that produced the bonanzas for modern fishermen.

The lake edge and bottom are one of Australia's most important laboratories in helping scientists solve the teasing problem of past climates. Recent research has shown that when the lake was at its maximum it was 36 metres deep and overflowed into the Yass River through its lowest lip. The last flowout was between

Lake George near Canberra is a famous 'disappearing' lake. It may be full of water and a haven for boating and fishing for a number of years, then it dries out and becomes good pasture land. The explanation is that it lies in a hollow with no creek outlets. In good rainfall years the water runoff fills the lake and after a series of dry years it empties through evaporation.

Three lakes make up this 11,000 hectare lagoon system. They are Myall, Boolanbyte and Broadwater Lakes.

26,000 and 19,000 years ago.

The present-day wealth of wildlife, including black swans and other waterbirds, would have made the lake a favoured haunt, particularly during the nesting season when vast numbers of waterbirds could have been gathered in frail boats.

During the great fillings sandy beaches formed when wind piled up material along the edges. A series of these occurred and studies in the sand have revealed Aboriginal stone implements, relics of the time (at least 15,000 years ago) when they camped there.

Unfortunately these sands are important to builders in Canberra where this material is in short supply. The lower beaches are under attack, as the older and higher levels have more clay mixed with the sand and are less attractive commercially.

The mud at the bottom of the lake is also a deposit of scientific importance. Pollens that gradually settled over the years can be taken from cores of this material and their study can reveal details of past climates. Pollen grains are not only resistant to decay but also have characteristics which allow botanists to identify the plant groups to which they belong.

When herbs dominate and trees and shrubs are uncommon a period of ice age conditions is indicated. The return of warm climates is shown by pollen similar to the harsher plantlife of the present day.

So from both a recreational and a scientific point of view Lake George is one of the important landforms of our country.

THE MYALL LAKES

The beauty of the Myall Lakes can best be appreciated by bushwalkers, or those who row quietly over the still waters. The reflections of swamp paperbarks and rusty gums, and the small paperbark and reed-clad islands, like scenes in a Chinese painting, create an overwhelming experience.

This complex on the mid-central coast of New South Wales is the largest system of partly fresh and partly brackish lakes in this state and of the 200 coastal lagoons along the eastern coast of Australia, most of which are used heavily for recreation,

it is one of the least polluted.

Three lakes make up this 11,000 hectare lagoon system. They are Myall, the largest and almost fresh, Boolanbyte, an interconnecting S-shaped stretch of water, and Broadwater, a brackish lake connected to the Myall River and the estuary of Port Stephens. To the north are two separate lakes, Smith's, which often opens directly into the sea to form a marine lagoon and therefore varies in salinity, and Wallis, which is a marine lagoon.

The expanse of water, stretching roughly northeast and southwest, is set in a landscape which offers both beauty and interest. Because of this a total of 17,000 hectares of land and water has been preserved as the Myall Lakes National Park.

Separated from it at the northeast corner by a small area of holiday homes is the Seal Rocks Nature Reserve, a number of offshore rocks which have the northernmost breeding colony of Australian fur seals. The establishment of family groups and the birth of the pups is a summer activity, although some seals are present all year. The nearby waters are the haunt of scuba divers who find the marine life rich and varied.

Even the least observant person can enjoy the wildlife in the national park and one ranger delights in telling the story of the camper who, after being warned he must remove his dog from the park as it disturbed the wildlife, retorted 'What wildlife?' At that moment a rustle in the branches overhead revealed a koala, peering down curiously.

In summer, when the inland lakes dry out, immense flocks of ducks and other waterbirds retreat to the more permanent coastal waters. At this time Myall Lakes becomes home to as many as half a million black ducks.

When did this chain of lakes along the coast form? The oscillation of the sea's edge during the various ice ages produced a variety of landforms along our coastlines. Today the lakes are separated from the sea by two series of dune ramparts, known as the inner and outer barrier systems.

The lakes themselves are fed from a catchment area of 540 square kilometres, most of which is forest with a section of cleared land. This explains why the waters are relatively unpolluted. Groundwater

feeds into the lakes from surrounding dunes and also helps create a number of smaller pondages and swamps between the dunes.

The low parabolic dunes lying on a hardpan below the surface making the inner barrier system were built some 35,000 years ago. As the sea retreated more lines of parallel dunes were formed and today they are covered with woodlands of rusty gum and some blackbutt.

The outer barrier was formed about 4,000 years ago and on these younger dunes, some of which are as high as 120 metres, stands of rusty gum have developed. Botanist Professor Roger Carolin thinks that these and other dunes at Norah Head are the best examples of this kind of woodland along the New South Wales coastline.

The two dune systems are an enormous scientific laboratory. When it was being examined with a view to creating a

Left and top:
Bald Rock is part of a giant granite dome. This landform and the surrounding country, with its associated landforms and wildlife, has been preserved as a national park.

Above:
This reserve near Glen Innes was called Stonehenge because of the strange stone sculptures produced by erosion.

national park it was stated, 'the area provides a unique opportunity on a world scale for research in the field of geological history. Few parts of the world have beach ridge formations, such as those between Hawks Nest and Seal Rocks, able to provide an insight into the variations in sea level which have occurred in relatively recent geological history'.

It was claimed with equal justice that 'no comparable area on the New South Wales coast contains the variety of coastal features, such as offshore islands, beaches, dunes, swamps, headlands, river and lakes, each with unique plant and wildlife associations'.

There must be few places where you can enjoy open sunlit heaths bright with flowers in winter and spring, continue on through impressive woodlands, to finally enter the dim coolness of rainforest at Mungo Brush.

The lakes, although not rich in fish, are famous for their prawns. Indeed, with a novel twist of the European rule on oysters, the fishermen hunt for prawns only when there is an 'r' in the month. Between September and April the prawners set their nets in a ritual which has been carried on for generations.

To add to the delights of inland waters and surrounding landscape there is also the pleasure of sand beaches stretching for 60 kilometres, while offshore there are the nature reserves of the Broughton Islands, a home of seabirds.

BALD ROCK

Almost 300 million years ago, during the period geologists named the Permian, our continent experienced changes, in both the balance of land and sea and the climate, which were of tremendous importance to Australia today. It was then that most of our coal and oil stores were created.

During this period a sea of ice covered much of southern Australia, while at the end of the era a convulsion produced the New England Fold Belt—a huge intrusion of granite pushed in from below—in the northeast corner of New South Wales. Such deep-seated rock masses are called batholiths. This term is derived from Latin and translates literally as deep stone, as 'lith' means stone and 'bath', deep.

No matter how deep a rock may be, the gnawing forces of hundreds of millions of years of erosion, and other changes in the earth's surface, can bring that rock mass to the surface, and Bald Rock near Tenterfield is one such fragment of the mass of granite.

Such rocks have always been popular picnic places in this district. There is Stonehenge, south of Glen Innes, where eroded rocks bear some resemblance to a natural Stonehenge. Nearby is the famous Balancing Rock where erosion has shaped a great sphere, seemingly precariously balanced on a granite base. To the east of Armidale are the Cathedral Rocks, while 30 kilometres north of Tenterfield is the vast dome of Bald Rock, 750 metres long and 500 metres wide. It is spectacular enough in area, but it also rises 200 metres above the surrounding country to give panoramic views in all directions.

Because of this striking landform slightly more than 2,000 hectares of the area has been set aside as a national park. It includes habitats ranging from forest to swampy heaths. Large marsupials such as the grey kangaroo, the prettyface, and swamp and black-striped wallabies appear, as well as the common wombat and the tiger quoll. Possibly the eastern quoll, a marsupial now extremely rare on the mainland, also exists there.

The major attraction, however, is Bald Rock, a reminder of that massive sea of granite which once lay buried deep in the earth.

THE WARRUMBUNGLES

'To the east a most stupendous range of mountains, lifting their blue heads above the horizon, bounded the view in that direction, and were distant at least seventy miles, the country appearing a perfect plain between us and them.'

So wrote Surveyor-General John Oxley in 1818 as he approached the Warrumbungles from the west.

As he came closer he wrote in more sombre mood '. . . its elevated points were extremely lofty, and of a dark, barren and gloomy appearance; . . .'

An appreciation of landscape is comparatively new, at least on the European scene. Even the word 'landscape' was new in the early 16th century. For the farmer, nature was the enemy, while for the traveller, wilderness

This vast dome called Bald Rock is 750 metres long, 500 metres wide, and 200 metres high.

was where wild beasts lurked.

Part of the change in attitude came with the romantic movement of the eighteenth and nineteenth centuries, but it was the American writer, Henry Thoreau, who helped realise the importance of mere enjoyment of the natural world in human survival in his phrase, 'In wildness is the preservation of the world'.

Oxley's comment that the mountains were surrounded by a 'perfect plain' is an interesting one and highlights the fact that national parks such as the Warrumbungles are in a sense 'islands' in a sea of change. This park of 18,000 hectares is a good example of the isolation from other areas of natural bush, which is one of the problems facing a park manager.

A great deal of thought is needed to make sure that the web of parks being set aside as samples of all the variety of landforms and wildlife Australia now contains will be linked by corridors of natural country along which wildlife can flow backwards and forwards as it has done since time immemorial.

The core of this park contains the remnants of volcanic activity which began just under 20 million years ago and ended 7 million years later when the volcanoes began a long sleep. The central section is the shield volcano from which poured fluid basalt as well as the more 'sticky' trachytic lavas. These spread, burying the ancient landscape under a 100 metre thick layer of volcanic rock. There were also

tremendous outpourings of solid material ranging from dust to 'bombs'—lumps of solid lava shot out like natural cannonballs.

All this helped form the rocks of the park. In addition, as particular vents slowly waned in activity, their cores held a plug of solid trachytic lava that was much harder than the rocks surrounding the break in the earth.

Also, below the surface, molten lava injected into cracks in the older rocks formed vertical walls. Geologists call these 'dykes', while those which intruded horizontally between old sediment layers are called 'sills'.

Such tough rocks remained behind when erosion removed the surrounding material already shattered by the force of the eruptions. Among the most famous of such landforms are Crater Bluff and Belougery Spire and the nearby Mount Wambelong at 1,206 metres. Perhaps the most remarkable is the great dyke aptly named The Breadknife—90 metres high, yet only a metre thick.

All of this volcanic activity produced a huge amphitheatre with lobes of rock radiating in all directions. The national park preserves only about a third of this with the volcanic rocks themselves occupying only about a third of the reserve. The bulk of the lower levels consist of sandstones, while most of the higher country, above 650 metres, is volcanic.

The sandstones are interesting as they

Above and over (pp. 28–9):
The Warrumbungle National Park preserves a great variety of volcanic landforms as well as fascinating wildlife. It is one of the most popular of the northern national parks and many walking trails make access to most landforms easy, even for the average walker.

Above left:
The Warrumbungles, the erosion remnants of volcanic rocks, rise abruptly from the surrounding plain. The tougher solidified lavas have resisted erosion, creating striking landforms such as Belougery Spire.

Far left:
The Breadknife rises sheer from the earth for 90 metres yet is only a metre wide. It is the remains of a volcanic dyke, the result of lava being squeezed into a vertical crack, where it hardened. The softer surrounding rock eroded away from the tougher material.

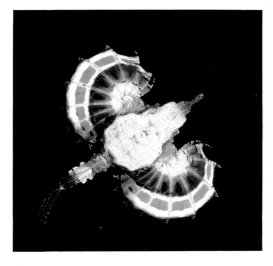

Top:
This soft coral (*Dendronephtha* sp.) is one of the fifty-seven species of coral to be found on Lord Howe Island.

Middle:
A splendid Hawkfish (*Cirrhitus splendens*).

Bottom:
This short Dragonfish (*Eurypegasus draconis*) is one of the 447 species of fish found on Lord Howe Island.

Right:
Admiralty Islands—part of the Lord Howe group of islands.

are of the Jurassic Age and part of the Great Artesian Basin. Being porous to water such rocks are part of the intake beds which supply the underground water of inland Australia. The total intake in this region stretches from Dubbo northward past Coonabarabran and on to Narrabri.

Such a combination of rocks has produced both fertile and barren soil. On the west the Warrumbungles face the semi-arid country of inland Australia and to the east the higher rainfall areas. The sandstone crumbles to poor soils on which live cypress pines as well as narrowleafed and mugga ironbarks and, when in season, a wealth of wildflowers.

On the richer volcanic soils particularly in sheltered areas, plants similar to those of the New England Tableland thrive. Pure stands of white box are a feature of the woodlands.

The animals of the Warrumbungles are as diverse as the plants. Koalas are found in suitable trees. Grey kangaroos are common, as well as euros and red-necked wallabies. Brush-tailed rock wallabies live on the rocky outcrops. In the past they were threatened by the competition of feral goats, but these are now being removed. Goats force rock wallabies from caves and overhangs and such shade is essential for survival as overheating in summer can be fatal.

Over the years a number of walking trails have been developed in the park and many can be covered in a few hours. The dramatic landforms, variable plantlife and abundant animals, including 170 kinds of birds, attract half a million visitors annually.

LORD HOWE ISLAND

'When I was in the woods among the Birds I cd, not help picturing to myself the Golden Age as described by Ovid . . .'
Surgeon Arthur Bowes, 16 May 1788.

'The most beautiful island in the world!' was the consensus of opinion on an international tour ship whose passengers were familiar with the world's favoured places.

In 1982 international opinion showed it agreed when the group of islands was added to the World Heritage List.

Upwellings from undersea volcanoes produced several undersea ridges to the east of Australia and on this volcanic base Lord Howe and its associated islands were built. A huge shield volcano erupted about 7 million years ago and continued its activity for some time. Then other forces took a hand. Weathering softened the harsh ridges, and seeds carried by wind and water, as well as by seabirds, clothed the rocks in a green mantle.

During those aeons of isolation the moulding hand of evolution produced a diversity of plants and animals unaffected by the interference of man as, apart from an occasional visit by the intrepid Polynesians, Lord Howe remained uninhabited.

Lieutenant Henry Lidgbird, on his way to Norfolk Island soon after the arrival of the First Fleet in Australia, saw this green jewel, and the nearby Balls Pyramid, in 1788.

The plants and animals on Norfolk Island when the first white settlers arrived were fascinating. A plant list prepared by botanist John Pickard of the National Herbarium in New South Wales shows 177 flowering plants, one-third of them found only on these islands.

The heavy rainfall, reaching 1,600 mm annually, and the good soil cover resulted in this rich development. Four major groups of plants are found only here, the best known being the palms, an important item of export to Australia and the rest of the world.

All of this plant variety is spread over a number of habitats, ranging from sea meadows in the shallow waters surrounding the island, across grassland to palm groves, gullies filled with ferns, and thick forests.

Screw palms, blue plums and scalybarks are among the taller trees, but the giant of all is the banyan fig, locally known by the appropriate name of 'walking tree' as it walks away from the parent trunk by sending out roots from the branches, that, once they grip the soil, become trees themselves that can rival the parent in size.

The beauty of the mountain top mossy forests rewards the hardy naturalists and bushwalkers who complete the difficult climb to the peaks.

The animals at present on the island are mainly birds and invertebrates, including many insects, but Lord Howe once had a remarkable reptile that apparently died out more than 20,000 years ago. This was a giant horned tortoise. Some scientists call it a turtle but it seems to have been an entirely land animal. Fossil remains have been found in a few places near the shoreline in the eolianites, rocks formed from coral sand were blown onto dunes by the wind and then cemented with lime.

The tortoise was apparently about 1·5 metres long and judging by its stumpy legs may have lived much as the giant tortoises of the Galapagos and Aldabra do today, feeding on plants.

Similar reptiles have been found as fossils in Queensland's Darling Downs and how these creatures arrived on this island some 500 kilometres to the east of the mainland is a problem. As the island was much larger in earlier times (it is 12 kilometres long now) other islands along the present submarine ridge may have served as stepping stones to the north and to the south. The animals and plants of the Lord Howe Island of today show strong relationships to those of eastern Australia, although there are also links with New Zealand to the south and New Caledonia and other islands to the north.

There have also been reports of land tortoises floating hundreds of kilometres out to sea so, judging by the toughness of present-day reptiles, it would seem quite possible that ancestors of the giant horned tortoise may have been blown eastward to their new home in a storm.

Why they died out is another mystery. Rising sea levels may have flooded so much of the island that the remaining population was no longer able to sustain itself, in much the same way as the Aboriginal population once living on Kangaroo Island was not able to remain viable once their land bridge was cut by the rising sea some 10,000 years ago. The extinct tortoise has two reptilian relatives today, a skink and a gecko lizard.

While other backboned animals may be missing, the birds more than make up for the deficiency. Lord Howe is truly an island of birds with some remarkable land-dwelling species and hosts of sea birds. The sea birds attract the most visitor-interest and the land birds draw the most scientific attention.

When the first Europeans arrived there were fifteen kinds of land birds and all but one were found only on this island group. Today the original fifteen has been reduced to only six and even two of these are in danger of extinction.

How did this disastrous situation come about? It must be realised that while islands are safe places for wildlife for a number of reasons, and many natural oddities like the dodo and the giant tortoises found them a haven when their relatives were disappearing on nearby continents, man's arrival usually leads to extinctions.

In an account of the birds of the Lord Howe Island group, Dr H. Recher points out that a study by the International Union for the Conservation of Nature noted that some 217 kinds of birds had become extinct in the last 400 years. Of these as many as 200 were island races or island species!

Disaster came swiftly to the birds of Lord Howe. Meat-hungry sailors and whalers first ravaged this island paradise, but the permanent damage began in 1834 with the first white settlement.

A stately ground bird called the white gallinule disappeared before 1844; the Lord Howe Island parakeet disappeared before 1870, and the island boobook owl before 1919. Other species were killed for food but most of the losses were due to the animals introduced by the settlers.

The one most destructive to the smaller birds came by accident when a ship called

Above:
Glorious beaches like Blinkey Beach abound on Lord Howe.

Left:
It is not difficult to see why Lord Howe and its associated islands were added to the World Heritage List in 1982.

the *Makambo* ran aground in 1918 and the rats on board deserted to the safety of the island. The species was the ship rat and it flourished at the expense of the wildlife. As it could climb trees no nests were safe from it and insects and lizards also became victims of this new predator.

Pigs gone wild were another predator. Their attack proved disastrous for the engaging woodhen, once widespread over the island but today restricted almost entirely to the mountaintops on the southern end. Feral cats and wandering dogs also added to the slaughter.

Fortunately a new day has dawned for the wildlife. The pigs have been destroyed, as well as many of the feral cats and the introduced masked owl has been culled. A successful breeding programme has produced more than fifty woodhen chicks and half of these have already been released into the wild. It seems likely that within a decade the woodhen, caught on the brink of extinction, will once more roam freely over the island.

A national park-type reserve on the southern end of the island, including

Mount Lidgbird which is 765 metres high, and Mount Gower at 866 metres, has been supplemented by another reserve at Malabar Range on the northern end.

Strict controls have at last been placed on the administration of the island so that its fragile beauty will, we hope, be kept intact.

The interest of Lord Howe Island continues beneath the water where the most southern coral reefs in the Pacific Ocean grow. Fifty-seven species of coral, almost all of them also found on the Great Barrier Reef, have been recorded.

Recent research indicates that these corals suffer from time to time from the killing effects of colder waters from the sub-Antarctic, but denuded reefs are re-colonised by larva riding in on tropical currents. The corals are not as diverse as those of the Great Barrier Reef, nor are the recorded 447 species of fish. These probably fluctuate in the same way and for the same reasons as the corals.

The marine wildlife can be explored in the 6 kilometre long lagoon sheltered from the prevailing winds on the western side of the island. There are two breaks in

Right:
Mt Gower, which is situated on the southern end of Lord Howe Island, is 866 metres high.

Far right:
Ball's Pyramid, a splendid volcanic landform whose pinnacle is 500 metres high.

the protecting reefs, and on the seaward side the water depth drops fairly sharply.

On the windward side of the island are three smaller, shallow-water reef areas. At one, Ned's Beach, the reef fish come close inshore and nibble bread held by excited visitors standing knee-deep in the water.

As well as the major lagoons and sandy beach areas there are other deeper reef areas, and these are gradually being explored, not only by scientists but also by scuba divers.

Myriads of sea birds feed on the rich marine life and a cruise to the outer islands is a naturalist's delight. At least eighteen species visit the group and ten nest on either the smaller islands or the main island.

Most spectacular are those abundant sea birds, the sooty terns, called 'wideawakes' because of their shrill call. An estimated 10,000 of them nest in season on Roche Island. They also nest on other islands, joined by masked boobies, wedgetailed shearwaters, common noddies and grey noddies.

Of great interest to visitors are the sea birds that nest on the main island. Visitors to Neds Beach walk through a large colony of fleshy-footed shearwaters and other colonies occur along the coast. That most beautiful of sea birds, the red-tailed tropic bird, nests on high rock ledges on the Malabar Ranges and the world's only nesting colony of the providence petrel is on the upper slopes of Mount Gower and Mount Lidgbird.

This petrel saved the settlers on nearby Norfolk Island from starvation in the days of the first occupation. Through greed they exterminated their 'bird of providence', but fortunately the colony on Lord Howe Island was found too late to suffer the same fate. The difficulty of reaching the nesting site explains their survival and today the island retains large groups of them. These petrels come to nest in early winter, arriving by day, an unusual behaviour pattern for sea birds such as shearwaters.

The small size of Lord Howe Island makes it easy to walk or cycle over most of it. The wealth of wildlife, both above and below water, makes it memorable; but the superb landscape, dominated by the towering peaks of Lidgbird and Gower, make it outstanding. From the mountaintops, dramatic landforms stand framed against the glittering green of the lagoons and the deeper blue of the sea. From the air the islands seem like a fairyland in a waste of ocean and must be one of the most beautiful island groups in the world.

BALLS PYRAMID

The pinnacle of Balls Pyramid towers 500 metres into the air, 19 kilometres southeast of the Lord Howe group of islands, part of the same volcanic landform which created Lord Howe.

The pyramid is a dramatic sight from every aspect as it stands on a wave-cut platform about 17 kilometres long and 14 kilometres wide which provides food and shelter for enormous numbers of fish and tourists are guaranteed a large catch here.

A multitude of sea birds, including about 1,000 sooty terns, as well as most of the species found nesting on Lord Howe, breed on the peak, the stately red-tailed tropic bird and masked booby adding to

the grandeur of the scene. A retinue of sea birds, anxious for food scraps, attend the boats fishing off the pyramid.

The Lord Howe group is under the legislative control of New South Wales. Through an oversight Balls Pyramid was not given such status in the early days of the colony so I claimed it on behalf of Australian conservationists. This led to counterclaims and the question was settled when the Premier of New South Wales asked an expedition which climbed to the top of the peak to plant a state flag there and declare it part of the Premier State—a lighthearted incident in the history of a colourful group of islands.

BURNING MOUNTAIN

There was exciting news from Scone in the year 1828—a stationhand some 20 kilometres north of this farming centre had seen a steady stream of smoke rising. It was obviously not a bushfire or an Aboriginal camp as it rose all day from the one place. Investigating, he found a whole hillock aflame, smoke pouring out from cracks in the rock. Tremendous heat came from the ground as well as the smell of sulphur dioxide so he hurried back with the news that a volcano was erupting. This news caused considerable interest in Sydney.

A Newcastle clergyman later brought the burning mountain to scientific notice, as did the explorer Major Thomas Mitchell. It was no young volcano but a steadily burning coal-seam. The local Aboriginals revealed that it had been burning for a very long time. Their word for fire was Wingen, and this was the name given to the site.

The coal itself is similar to the beds found at Singleton, a mineral treasure created in swamps hundreds of millions of years ago.

Wingen is the only natural burning coal-seam in Australia and the puzzle is how it caught alight, as outcrops of coal are found in many parts of our continent and bushfires must have passed across them many times in our history. Possibly it was the way the coal outcropped, or a case of spontaneous combustion. Water combining with the iron pyrites may have produced so much heat from chemical activity that finally the coal burst into flames.

Complex chemical reactions are certainly taking place deep in the earth as the surface of the hilltop is liberally coated with solid yellow sulphur. This was probably turned into vapour by the heat, then cooled back to solid on contact with the air at the surface.

The heat from the burning has altered the rocks so that they look like slag from a furnace, showing dull reds, dark greys and blacks. The blue smoke drifting over the scene contains a choking gas familiar to all those who have spent days in a school chemical laboratory.

Traces of old fires can be seen in a hollow at Little Burning Mountain. Since then it has moved steadily up the side of Burning Mountain to its present position. Great cracks have opened in the earth and the dozen or so plumes of smoke pouring out of holes in the ground, together with the heat radiating from the earth, make this an eerie scene.

If the present rate of progress has been constant, then the coal-seam began to burn about 3,000 years ago. The fire will go out some time in the future as a fault has cut across the seam and the coal-bed stops abruptly on the southeast edge of the mountain.

It has not only served as a tourist spot. The Reverend C. P. N. Wilton wrote in 1830, 'Even this fiery mountain, the terror of the native and the wonder of the Colonist, has not been without benefit to the neighbouring settler—its sulphurous and aluminous products combined, having been successfully applied in the cure of the scab in sheep.'

Not only in sheep; an advertisement in the *Sydney Mail* of 1902 told of the virtues of 'Winjenna' remedies. These included soap at ninepence a cake and ointments for treating sore eyes, scalds and other ailments.

The mining of sulphur ended in 1964, and today this 500 metre hill with its 3 metre thick coal-seam, and 57 hectares of surrounding country, has been declared a nature reserve. The vegetation is grey box and rough-barked apple woodland, with open country containing both native and introduced pastures.

THE BLUE MOUNTAINS

As the first white settlers of Sydney pushed westward in search of better pastures they saw on the horizon a line of mountains. A few resolute farmers became explorers and tried to find a breach in those misty blue hills, but they were baffled by a new kind of landform.

Using their European experience they followed up rivers hoping to reach the top of the hill. Then it should have been a simple matter to look for another valley leading in the opposite direction.

These Australian mountains were different, as was to be expected in this upside-down world. The rivers became creeks and ended abruptly at 200 metre high vertical walls.

At last Blaxland, Lawson and Wentworth learned the trick of following the ridge lines and crossed the ranges in 1813. Two years later hardworking convicts made a permanent breach with a road to Bathurst and the rich western slopes and plains were open for settlement.

The Blue Mountains, a forward spur of the Great Dividing Range and the mountain backbone of eastern Australia, have remained relatively untouched since those early times, except for some hardy

Above:
The Blue Mountains, west of Sydney, earned their name because of the blue haze that always envelops the area and gives it a characteristic colour when it is seen from a distance.

Top:
The Burning Mountain formed when a coal seam caught alight long before the coming of the white settlers. Cracks are produced by tremendous heat drying the topsoil.

Left:
The surface colours of Burning Mountain are produced by the heating of the soil and also from deposits of sulphur.

Above:
Wildflowers near Katoomba in the Blue Mountains.

Right:
The Jamieson Valley in the Blue Mountains.

Far right:
Cyclorama Point in the Jamieson Valley, Blue Mountains.

farmers and those who built holiday homes there so that they could enjoy the bracing air when summer brought sultry heat to the lowlands of Sydney.

The history of the rocks of the Blue Mountains is similar to that of the Sydney Basin. The Kosciusko Uplift of a million years ago raised this section of eastern Australia, tilted the western edge of the basin, and in these new highlands the rivers began their task of reducing the mountains back to a plain in the never-ending cycle of erosion and uplift.

In this process of cutting through the layers of sandstone, incredible gorges were created by the rivers. Even when the great English naturalist, Charles Darwin, was travelling over the range he stared in bewilderment at this immense work of nature and wrote, 'To attribute these hollows to the present alluvial action would be preposterous'.

Even when one understands the geological process, a chasm as huge as that of the Grose Valley is stunning in its impact. Yet such rivers, working over aeons of time, are the tools that gouge such valleys from the rocks.

In this century these valleys in the mountains are no longer an irritating barrier to the west but a target in themselves. Generation after generation of bushwalkers have revelled in the challenge of scree slope and chasm, with at journey's end the delight of camping in towering bluegum forests on the banks of ferny creeks.

Here shy lyrebirds stalk food on the forest floor and bowerbirds call harshly as they tend their amazing display structures luring female birds, not only with the bower itself and its painted inner walls, but also with song and dance.

What seemed to the first white settlers to be a great misfortune, came with the whirligig of time to be regarded as Sydney's greatest good fortune! What other great city can boast it has the forest primeval almost at its doorstep?

The settlers' axes removed most traces

of the original bush near the city for farms, but the combination of a rugged landscape and relatively poor soil saved this wilderness. State governments set aside national parks over the choicest pieces, but the greatest dedication has taken place in the last few years. The present NSW Premier, Neville Wran, said when announcing the latest national park to be declared that he would probably be remembered in the future because of the national parks he had helped to create as a backdrop to Sydney.

Huge is the only word that can be used to describe the 160,000 hectares of the Blue Mountains National Park and with the Kanangra-Boyd and the Colo-Wollomi parks there is a grand total of nearly one and a half million hectares of unspoiled bushland! An amazing variety of heaths, mallees, towering forests, waterfalls, plunging sandstone walls, and a wealth of animal life delights every visitor.

Above all, the formidable landforms offer a challenge to those who want more than a pleasant walk along the abundant graded pathways. For them there is the keen pleasure of steeping themselves in the wilderness to find refreshment far from any visible works of man.

THE THREE SISTERS

It is remarkable that these three pinnacles of sandstone were regarded as female, when in strength, craggy contour and size they appear to typify traditional masculine stereotypes!

The Three Sisters are the major feature of the popular lookout called Echo Point at Katoomba in the Blue Mountains. They are residuals of erosion over many thousands of years and joint planes have allowed rocks to tumble into the valley below as weathering worked along these lines of weakness.

Echo Point is the best place to appreciate the landforms of the area. From here there is a view of Cox's Valley,

while in every direction can be seen the harder sandstones and claystones which lie upon the softer Permian sediments.

Although the cliff faces are usually only about 250 metres high the creeks lie in much deeper valleys, often as much as 700 metres below the clifftops. This depth, with a dense growth of forests, stands in sharp contrast to the bare sandstone rocks. The golden light of the late afternoon, the cobalt-blue haze and the green of the plants together produce a magnificence which has become world famous.

On the other side of the plateau from Govett's Leap, which is one of the many gauzy waterfalls that drift down to the valley below after heavy rain, can the awe-inspiring Grose Valley be enjoyed. Full appreciation comes from taking one of the walking tracks that allows a close

The northern approach to the park is about 16 kilometres from the Jenolan Caves and access at the southern end is by 80 kilometres of road from Oberon.

The feature that attracts many visitors is the view of the Kanangra Walls. From here Mount Colong, a huge residual of sandstone with a capping of basalt, can be seen. This region was the site of a great conservation controversy a decade ago. The conservation battle was finally won and the group involved continued as the Colong Society, devoted to the protection of wilderness.

The Kanangra Walls are a mixture of rocks from the Permian period when the great coal-seams which provided so much wealth for New South Wales were laid down. Indeed, they are an ideal pictorial textbook for the study of sediment formations, with the older quartzites as

Right:
Many of the better-known landforms, which are eroded out of sandstone, have popular names, such as the Three Sisters.

Far right
Kanangra Walls in the Blue Mountains, south of the Jenolan Caves, is a dramatic valley slope carved out of the series of rocks of the area.

examination of the rocks themselves and the most spectacular views are across the valley.

Areas in Mount Wilson come as a surprise as here a capping of basalt allowed rich soils to develop and so luxuriant forests and stately trees grow well.

THE KANANGRA WALLS

About fifteen years ago a conservation battle raged in the Blue Mountains as the state government of the time planned to mine limestone in the heart of one of the few remaining wilderness areas close to Sydney.

This was probably the first time conservationists were able to organise a campaign efficiently and obtain support from a wide range of the public. Victory came when the disputed area and its surroundings were declared as the Kanangra-Boyd National Park in 1969. Its 57,000 hectares remain very much as it was in the days of the first white settlement.

the base rocks and the shales and sandstones of the coal measures lying above.

When such sediments are laid down on an older eroded surface, their angle of deposition may be different from the rocks that were formed before. Geologists say they lie unconformably and the line of their meeting is called an unconformity—this can be studied with binoculars from a convenient viewing place created on a high point above the valley.

JENOLAN CAVES

Perhaps primeval memories help explain the fascination we still feel for caves. Here is natural shelter from rain, wind and cold, and a home where a fire could be kept burning for warmth and light at night.

The Jenolan Caves in the Blue Mountains are among the most attractive and the most popular of all the Australian cave systems. Part of their charm is the journey to the site through most of the landforms that have made this part of

Above:
The Jenolan Caves, New South Wales.

Right:
Kanangra Walls in the Blue Mountains.

Australia famous. On the drive from Mount Victoria, after the descent of the western slopes of the Blue Mountains, a 15 kilometre stretch of road reveals dramatic cliffs. The steep drive into the caves area also allows a view of untouched wilderness.

The Aboriginals would have known the caves. Indeed one underground cavern was called Skeleton Cave after the discovery of an Aboriginal inhabitant who died there.

Legend has it that it became the hideout for a bushranger after white settlement, but the recorded history of that period of the 1830s reveals nothing about such a marauder.

A local farmer, James Whalan, discovered the cave system and it became very popular, people coming from the Sydney region and from the western town of Bathurst to see the natural wonder. It was said at the time that the way to the caves could be found quite easily by the discarded fragments of stalactites and stalagmites, broken off as mementoes by uncaring visitors.

The NSW State Government, well aware of the caves' potential value, set aside the first reserve in the area as long ago as 1866, 13 years before the declaration of Royal National Park.

Unfortunately in those early days the construction of roads and access paths led to some spoiling of the natural beauty.

The caves of Jenolan were dissolved out of limestones laid down in a sea of some 400 million years ago, then exposed as a bed of rock which today outcrops as a line of limestone running north and south with the caves being concentrated in a 5 kilometre strip.

Three streams cut across this mass of limestone; one of them helped create the Grand Arch. The arch was once a cave that collapsed through erosion and is now 140 metres long, 24 metres high and some 70 metres wide, and the main road runs underneath it.

The Devil's Coachhouse, which is almost as large, leads to Carlotta Arch which forms a magnificent frame for Blue Lake. In all, 22 major caves have been found and there are a number of smaller ones. Guided tours are taken through eight of them.

Shawl formations developing when the seepage is along a crack are common and produce striking effects when they are coloured by mineral impurities. The stalactites grow steadily from the roof to meet the more solid stalagmites growing from the floor. When they meet they form

Far left, top and left:
The Jenolan Caves were dissolved out of the limestones concentrated in a 5 kilometre long strip in the Blue Mountains. Ground water charged with carbonic acid dissolves limestone to form caves. As the years pass and the air circulation improves the limestone dissolved in the ground water comes out of solution to fill in the cavern it created aeons before.

The deposited lime may shape spires, hanging spikes or shawls, often coloured by impurities, and these formations attract thousands of visitors.

pillars, although none reach the 3 metre diameter of some pillars in Tasmanian caves.

All these create remarkable forms that tempt the fanciful into finding resemblances wherever they look. Imperial Cave, discovered in 1879 boasts the following list of caves: The Woolshed, Model Chamber, Pine Forest, Shawl Cave, Confectioner's Shop, Lot's Wife, Grand Stalactites, Alabaster Column, Nellie's Grotto, Fairies' Bower, Crystal Palace, Bridal Veil, Gem of the West and Underground River. Others hold The Cathedral, Music Room, Mafeking, Angel's Wing, Cloth of Gold, Goblin's Basin and the Bath of Venus. This florid list is an essential part of the tourist literature!

There is a wide variety of wildlife in the nearby forest. One particular species, the rock warbler, is found only in the Sydney region and is a favourite through its behaviour pattern of hanging its nest from the roof of a cave. With the coming of man, some birds have accepted his buildings as artificial caves and built their nests inside them!

Brush-tailed rock wallabies were once abundant in the rocky outcrops but their numbers have dropped in recent years. Brushtail possums linger around the buildings which house the visitors and over the years have become very tame.

Caverns such as Jenolan would seem easy to conserve but there are problems. Access for visitors must be provided skillfully. Most of Australia's better-known cave resorts have suffered from amateur planning in the past. The numbers of visitors also create problems in terms of changing the cave environment.

It was found necessary to steam clean some of the caves at Jenolan to remove the flotsam resulting from 100 years of tourist visitation. The very presence of artificial light, by providing energy for plant growth allows algae and similar lowly plants to flourish and their remains disfigure the beauty of the cave formations.

Even more damaging in the long term are road and other works which may change drainage patterns and alter the levels of water tables. Both of these created the cave scenery and their continued health is essential to the survival of the cave system as a living landform.

THE WILLANDRA LAKES REGION

The most monotonous of landscapes, may, with greater knowledge, suddenly become a place of discovery, excitement and wonder. '. . . the Willandra Lakes belong not only to the heritage of all Australians, but they merit world heritage status as a unique document of ice-age environment and testimony to the antiquity of Aboriginal Australians'. *The Heritage of Australia*, 1981.

In 1982 the Willandra Lakes Region was added to the World Heritage List with the complete support of the New South Wales Government. The importance of the region first became known to science in the late 1960s and since then world interest has escalated. The nomination put before the World Heritage Committee was able to claim the '. . . system stands in the same relation to the global documentation of the culture of early Homo sapiens as the Olduvai Gorge relates to hominid origins.'

Part of the area was already reserved as the Lake Mungo National Park while the rest of the region is under the control of the Western Land Commission under a leasehold system. The value of leasehold over freehold is that the government can enforce conditions which protect the quality of the country, for either its plant and animal values, or as in this case, for its cultural heritage.

Why is this semi-arid part of Australia so valuable in world terms? Far from the nearest seas of the Southern Oceans, even though only 70 metres above the present sea level, the region has been stable in terms of earth movement. The rivers and creeks wind slowly on their journey to the sea along a gradual slope, so erosion is not severe. The coming of the white settlers with their flocks accelerated erosion; yet, paradoxically, it also brought hidden treasures to light. This happened when a dune on the shore of Lake Mungo was stripped of 30 per cent of its surface by overgrazing. Fortunately dunes on other lakes are entire and almost certainly contain more treasures for study by the archaeologists of the future.

In 1969 the Lake Mungo 'Eve' was found. A young woman, judging from her remains, she was burnt, and then her bones were crushed and buried in a pit, in an obvious ceremonial ritual. The bones

were dated as being approximately 26,000 years old, making Willandra the oldest cremation site in the world.

Other amazing discoveries followed. Only 500 metres away Dr J. M. Bowler found a tall man, also burnt but laid out in his grave with hands clasped. His body, and the pit itself, were deeply coated with red ochre. The bones were dated as 30,000 years in age and lumps of red ochre 32,000 years old were found nearby.

Archaeologist Professor John Mulvaney pointed out that the manner of burial and the use of ochre showed deep spiritual beliefs. Similar burial rituals have been discovered in palaeolithic Europe and so we find human populations linked spiritually although divided by thousands of kilometres of land and sea.

Further studies in the eroded lunette of Lake Mungo have helped establish a deeper knowledge of early man and his way of life in the lush surroundings of these freshwater lakes. Artefacts also revealed those sadder days when the waters disappeared and the Aboriginals had to turn from the once-rich supplies of mussels, fish and other wildlife to gathering the seeds of grasses. They crushed these on slabs of sandstone recently found on these ancient campsites.

The presence of ochre shows more than aesthetic impulses. In this land of lakes and sand dunes there would have been no source of this mineral. We know from the trading patterns of the present-day Aboriginals that such iron ores used as ceremonial paints were traded over thousands of kilometres. It is probable that the red ochre used on Lake Mungo 'Eve' and 'Adam' came from as far afield as Parachilna in South Australia, a rich mine for the Aboriginals of southeastern Australia.

All this conjures up a picture of the Australian world of those far-off times, of a thriving community, living in a lush landscape and busy, not only with hunting, food gathering and trading, but with rituals of the Dreamtime. It also appears to have been a peaceful period with plentiful food and rich in ceremony.

The Willandra Lakes, although far from the seashore, were affected by the climatic changes which heralded the coming and going of ice ages. In discussing many of our landforms we have mentioned the changes caused in the last million years by the waxing and waning of ice sheets, formed and melted by changes in the world temperature of a few degrees.

It must be appreciated that floating ice has no effect on the sea levels of the world. An icecube melting in a glass makes no difference to the level of the water as the solid ice shrinks slightly in melting and fills exactly the space the block displaced.

It is the ice and snow locked onto continents that is important. It has been estimated that if all the water held bound on Antarctica were to melt through a rise in temperature, then sea levels around the world would rise about 100 metres—with catastrophic effect.

Today the Lakes are part of a river system beginning with the Willandra Billabong Creek which itself is part of the Lachlan river, and this in turn flows into the Murrumbidgee, then into the Murray-Darling system and finally the southern ocean.

This interconnected line of lakes and streams once flowed steadily, filling some lakes to depths of 10 metres. In this area of about 6,000 square kilometres of sand dunes and other soils there was at that time 1,000 square kilometres of fresh water. Wildlife flourished as richly as it does in the present Murray River, the wetlands of Kakadu, and the banks of the Darling.

An important, even dominant, item was the freshwater mussel—a mollusc women and children gathered in abundance by wading in the shallow waters of a lake or diving a few metres to the bottom of deeper lakes. Huge piles of these shells discarded where they were eaten show a pattern of food-gathering found around many Australian waterways.

Along seashores the freshwater mussel was replaced by its marine relative, the cockle, called ugari or pipi by the Aboriginals.

In those days, as they do today in similar rivers and lakes, the waters teemed with fish including the golden perch and Murray cod. The Aboriginals lived well in this land of milk and honey for about 2,000 generations; an almost unimaginable time compared with the few generations of white settlement.

At this time the main wind system was westerly and the waves in the lakes pushed up heaps of sand on the eastern shorelines, forming the masses of material we call lunettes. This building began at least 40,000 years ago, peaked between 18,000 and 16,000 years ago, and came to a standstill 15,000 years ago when the great dry caused the waters of the lakes to shrink and disappear.

The streams dried out to intermittent pools and then became nothing more than dry channels, which caused hard times to fall on the Aboriginals. Change would have been gradual, the shrinking population keeping pace with the shrinking food supplies. Finally the people would have become nomads and drifted across the dry country.

How do we know so exactly the story of our early history? Scientists such as Dr J. M. Bowler have been able to interpret past climates, river systems and dune shifts from a study of the present-day landforms, although the sequence of events at Lake Mungo and the other nearby lakes was much more complex than the brief summary given here.

Scientists rely on the remains of artefacts used in the hunt and the even more important rubbish discarded around the numerous camps for evidence of man's occupation in this region. But by a lucky chance the most exciting material of all, the human remains, were discovered.

The waters which fed the chain of lakes came from the eastern Highlands and their gradual drying up shows evidence of an advance of the central deserts, not only into western New South Wales, but also into southern Victoria and the northeast of Tasmania at a time when Bass Strait had become dry land.

All these changes are a key to the unravelling of the reasons for the creation of the landforms of the Willandra Lakes Region. Today the country is less barren and the soils have been stabilised by plantlife, which includes belts of mallee and cypress pines on sandy areas.

The wildlife, although abundant in terms of an arid landscape, has shrunk from those lush days of long ago when the Aboriginals were able to hunt for hare-wallabies, boodies, hairy-nosed wombats, and Tasmanian devils and Tasmanian tigers—both of these long gone from the mainland.

Willandra was also the home of a giant 3 metre tall kangaroo, now known only as fossils. Hunting by early man, together with the gradual drying of the continent, probably led to the extinction of this and other giant marsupials.

Today the person who explores on foot can appreciate the wonder of the prickly ramparts of spinifex, the beauty in a shingleback lizard, and the charm of gawky emus wandering in a landscape familiar to them for thousands of years.

The camper waking at sunrise can see the beauties of the eroded lunette dune of Lake Mungo as in the slanting light it appears to rear like an ancient wall. The first white settlers called them the Walls of China, in tribute to the indefatigable Chinese immigrants who turned to labouring after the gold ran out. They built the great woolshed of Mungo Station in 1869, (only nine years after the ill-fated Burke and Wills party crossed this Willandra country) using locally sawn logs from the pine that still grows plentifully in the sandy country surrounding the Willandra region.

Queensland

THE GREAT BARRIER REEF

Here is undoubtedly the largest structure built by any living creature, including man! In any modern list of the seven natural wonders of the world, this 2,000 kilometre long maze of reefs built underwater by coral polyps would have a place.

Coral polyps are found here in incredible diversity with about 400 species already identified. Darting in and out of the sheltering coral arms, as well as swimming along the deeper channels and in the areas of inland sea, are about 1,500 kinds of fish and six species of turtle. There are forty kinds of seabirds, more than half of them nesting on the islands of the reef.

Few of us have not daydreamed of being marooned on a coral island where warm seas and trade winds would make life idyllic. In the shallow lagoons fish would be caught and shells gathered. The marvels of the underwater life would be enjoyed and an occasional walk in the sunshine along a sandy beach would make the day perfect.

Dreams rarely survive reality, yet a coral cay on the Great Barrier Reef is a place where they can come true.

Where coral reefs flourish today, 15,000 years ago the Aboriginals would have walked on dry land hunting wallabies and other creatures of the coastal forests. For during the last ice age, the shoreline would have retreated to the east, leaving much of the continental shelf as dry land.

With the melting of the world's ice caps, beginning some 15,000 years ago and coming to an end about 6,000 years ago, sea levels around the world rose some 45 metres, shrinking the Australian continent by about one-third and bringing back to the present Great Barrier Reef region those warm shallow waters in which corals can thrive. So, on the skeletons of coral reefs which had flourished in earlier times, a new reef was created.

Reef polyps build living homes in great colonies, often containing tens of thousands of animals. For this they need clear waters with temperatures between 20 and 30 degrees Celsius and, ideally, depths of between 5 and 28 metres. The reason is that in these polyp tissues are microscopic plants that add to the vigour of their growth. Sunlight is essential for plants to survive and below 28 metres the brightness of the sea begins to fade into the permanent darkness of the sea depths. No plants can live there so the kinds of polyps which only live in colonies and need plants in their bodies are restricted to the brighter areas near the surface.

The animals that live in these deeper waters either use them as a retreat during the day, rising to the surface to forage by night, or survive by scavenging the steady rain of bodies which pours down from where life flourishes in the warmth and sunlight. Here they are nourished by nutrients sucked up from the depths by the surge of ocean waters backwards and forwards, moved by the pull and the push of the tides.

Channels that carry this rush of water at speeds of 1·5 metres a second are common and can pull water up from depths of 140 metres. The cool, nutrient-rich waters await the stirrings of nature to release their invigorating material back to the cycle of life on the coral reef. This material is first used by the outer-reef creatures so it is here that coral growth is most rapid.

The present veneer of living coral grows on a platform of rubble up to 5 metres deep made from the skeletons of their recent ancestors, but the whole area has an ancient history. It is believed the first coral reefs began to grow in this region some 25 million years ago.

At this time earth movements caused the great arching upwards of the eastern highlands, creating mountains. On the seaward side a vast trough developed.

In waters free of sediment, corals could flourish. Their greatest period of growth began about two million years ago and, after the swinging to and fro of the sea's edge during the various ice ages, the present reef developed some time between 15,000 and 6,000 years ago.

The Great Barrier Reef is the largest coral reef system in the world and the largest structure built by any living creatures, including man.

Left:
Heron Island is a true coral cay at the southern end of the reef and a popular tourist resort where underwater life can be seen at low tide.

Present research puts 8,000 years as the main age of our modern reef that grows on a foundation of the more ancient corals.

There are three major sections of the modern Great Barrier Reef. At the southern end, just north of Fraser Island, is Lady Elliot cay, once a rich source of guano, then home to a lighthouse that helped ships find a way through the treacherous puzzle of reefs. Today it is a new tourist resort.

Further to the north are the Capricorn and Bunker groups of cays which have delighted holidaymakers for nearly one hundred years. For tourists these are the closest approach to the coral islands of fiction. Here are reefs that can be walked over at low tide, pools for snorkelling in at high tide, and fish as colourful as can be found anywhere in the world. Scuba divers can enjoy the 'bommies', masses of living coral rising from the depths, in seas which are perhaps 150 metres deep.

Here too can be seen the platform or patch reefs that grow straight out of the depths.

The coral cays are pieces of land

green or loggerhead turtle to appear above the silvery surface of the sea and make her way ashore. The turtle has a laborious and gasping climb to the sand above highwater mark before beginning the old ritual of nest building and egglaying, done in a pattern of behaviour begun in the mists of time some 60 million years ago; a pattern so successful it has continued unchanged.

Nothing else I have experienced brings home to me more deeply the feeling of community with nature; the belief that I too am part of a living thread which stretches back to the first creative steps which took place 3,500 million years ago.

The relentless hunting of turtles in most parts of the world means that we have a unique sanctuary as all our species are now protected.

The middle section of the reef has near the coast many mainland-type islands that have become important holiday resorts. They are not coral cays, but old headlands converted into islands by the rising sea. Here, as well as platform reefs, are fringing reefs which began in the shallow water of the islands and grew

snatched from the sea by the gradual accumulation of fragments of rock thrown high on a reef. Over the years other debris is added, including sand from the shallow water. Seeds drift in, borne by wind or water or carried on the feet of birds, and from these start the first assemblages of land plants. Finally arrive the trees, including beach sheoak, beach pandanus and birdlime trees—three species which are now a feature of coral cays such as Heron Island.

Also to these islands came the marine turtles, free from the need of land except when the female must come ashore to lay her eggs deep in the sand. Safe from salt water they incubate in the warmth of the soil.

There can be few activities as exciting as sitting quietly on a moonlit beach watching for the first dark shape of a

outwards to provide protective shields to the land.

In the northern section the water is shallower—no more than 36 metres deep. Here there are mainland-type islands and also coral cays. Some of them have developed mangrove communities, a feature not found in southern cays.

The reef has played an important part in human history, details of which we are still discovering. The first people to visit the inshore reefs in the northern section and land on the offshore islands, were the Aboriginals. They built outrigger canoes which could hold hunting parties that supplied mainland camps with food. So plentiful was the supply that the main bases would move very little, and every two or three years great gatherings would take place. It was then that the young men would gain a new 'skin' as they were

Far left:
Coral sea on the northern Great Barrier Reef.

Left:
Garbage sharks on Heron Island.

Above:
Polyp coral, *Tubastrea Cup.*

51

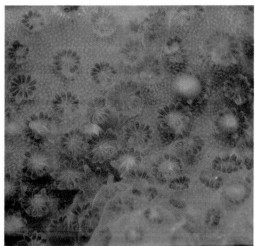

Top:
Anemone fish.

Middle:
Coral reproducing.

Bottom and right:
Corals of the Great Barrier Reef. This huge area of
coral reefs extends some 2,000 kilometres along the
Queensland coast. Some 2,500 individual reefs make
up the largest single structure built by animals,
including the cities of humans. The Great Barrier
Reef is the world's largest and most complex of all
living coral reefs and is a World Heritage area.
About 400 species of corals have been recorded.

Over (pp. 54–5):
Turtles are clumsy on land but strong swimmers. In
the sea they move rapidly by means of powerful
flippers.

initiated into adulthood.

Perhaps the first navigators from the northern world to explore these waters were the Chinese who certainly visited Timor and could easily have travelled eastward on the monsoons and returned on the southeast trade winds. The Spanish and Portuguese may also have come; and some maps of the mid-sixteenth century certainly show a remarkably accurate outline of the east coast.

To know the land with certainty Europe had to wait for the arrival of Captain Cook in 1770. As he pushed his way northward, charting the coastline, he had little inkling of this vast natural coral wonderland until he actually ran his ship on it, near what is now Cooktown.

Cook was lucky as his ship wasn't wrecked, but many other captains were not as fortunate and the wreckage of many ships is scattered along the length of the reef.

In the first days of white settlement many of the islands were mined for guano, the droppings of countless generations of seabirds, so vital to the farmers of Australia for fertiliser. Hunting for a marine mammal called the dugong began and then came fishing for turtle, pearling, and the gathering of trepang, a sea slug relished by gourmets in Asia. There were other industries, but in recent times, although fishing is of great importance, the main one is tourism.

From all over the world, as well as from Australia, visitors flooded in to see this greatest of coral reefs and

Right:
Coral cays in the Capricorn Group of the Great Barrier Reef. These are true coral islands built up from fragments of coral and other debris washed up by the sea.

Below:
Lizard Island, a national park near the northern end of the Great Barrier Reef Marine Park, is famed for its fringing coral reefs.

conservationists realised that only expert management could keep this natural wonder unspoiled.

In 1975 The Great Barrier Reef Marine Park Act was passed and an Authority created to manage all the waters of the Reef. The Queensland Government has control of the mainland-type islands and the seventy-one coral cays. Most of the islands have been reserved as national parks.

This reservation has produced the largest marine park anywhere in the world. It must be remembered, however, that such marine parks are not national parks in the accepted sense of the word. Old activities, including fishing, continue, but after scientific study and public discussion, sections rich in coral diversity and with a wealth of other wildlife are selected as wilderness zones and kept inviolate; they are, in effect, 'national marine parks'.

It is a grand concept and the hundreds of thousands of conservationists who worked to make this dream a reality have every reason to be proud of their efforts.

Perhaps their greatest moment came when the Great Barrier Reef was accepted as part of the World Heritage. This world conservation organisation has put a seal of international approval on an area which contains the largest single collection of coral reefs in the world and which holds the most diverse ecosystem known to man.

Although the reef is Australian property in terms of international law, in ethical terms we are acting only as trustees for the rest of the world. Let us hope we can hand on this natural wonderland in even better condition than we found it, for the enjoyment not only of future generations of Australians but for people everywhere.

THE GREAT SANDY ISLANDS

One of the attractions of the Queensland coastline is its wealth of sand. These huge deposits of sand continue northward from the Gold Coast to the region that contains Stradbroke, Moreton and Fraser Islands. Here the sand diminishes as the protecting Great Barrier Reef blocks it from reaching the coast in large

Above and right:
Turtles come ashore usually under cover of darkness to lay eggs. The female laboriously digs a huge pit. At the bottom of it she digs a smaller cylindrical hole in which to lay a number of eggs. They look like glistening ping-pong balls but do not bounce quite as high. Egglaying over, the turtle covers them with sand and returns to the sea where she is safe.

59

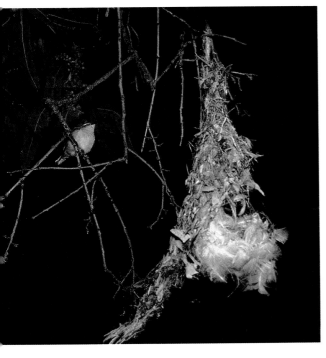

Above:
A sunbird with its hanging nest. This is one of the colourful birds of Queensland.

Top right:
Sooty terns nest in thousands of Michaelmas Cay near Cairns. The single egg is laid in a slight hollow in the sand, the bird making no attempt to create a nest lining.

Right:
The Heron Island reef from the air. Heron Island is one of the major tourist resorts of the southern end of the Great Barrier Reef.

Far right:
Black noddy terns nest on coral cays. They are very tame and may be approached closely before they fly off.

quantities. Yet there are still sandy beaches and they increase in size until on the eastern side of Cape York massive sand drifts dominate the coastal scenery as well as travelling well inland.

The high-energy wave coastline of Queensland stretches from the New South Wales border to the northern part of Fraser Island. In this section a steady drift of sand is pushed along by the southeast trade winds, and islands and spits grow longer in a northerly direction. The most spectacular and best known of these are the spit at Southport and Cape Bowling Green near Ayr.

North of Fraser Island is a low-energy wave coastline as the Great Barrier Reef dampens wind effects and there is less northerly drift. It is believed that most of this sand developed from the weathering and erosion of the Great Dividing Range rocks, particularly in the New England region. From these sandstones and granites came the silica that remained unchanged (as this mineral is chemically

inert) during the slow movement to the sea and the following northward drift caused by the tradewinds.

Also carried along in this mass of silica we call sand were heavy minerals. The valuable minerals here include zircon, rutile, ilmenite with monazite, and garnet, and combined with other materials they make up the famous black sands of the east coast. For many years the bulk of the world's supply of rutile and zircon came from the beaches of eastern Australia.

Battles were fought between miners keen to reap these riches for export and conservationists, who saw beautiful beach and dune country, sometimes clothed with tall trees and beautiful wildflowers, being smoothed to a dull uniformity by mining.

The islands' individual beauty and the pleasant winter climate have meant that a few places have been 'loved to death' by the numbers of people who have come to enjoy them. Yet good management can change this and some areas have been

saved. Two of the best known are Cooloola and Fraser Island; although the latter, not being entirely a national park, still suffers from unrestricted use.

Fraser Island

'Fraser Island is to the sandmasses of the World, what the Great Barrier Reef is to the coral reefs of the World' is the enthusiastic claim of some scientists.

Fraser Island is the largest sand island in the world, being just over 120 kilometres long and between 25 and 50 kilometres wide, and with an area of over 160,000 hectares. Its link with the mainland is shown by the narrowness of the Great Sandy Strait dividing it from Queensland and the fact that its southern tip is only 2 kilometres from the mainland shore.

It is made almost entirely of material deposited in the last few million years. The sand lies upon a bedrock 30 metres below the present sea level, the only outcrops of hard rock being in the Indian Head-Waddy Point area on the east coast where volcanic material makes a minor break in the great sea of sand.

On the older bedrock sand has been heaped into great dunes, some as high as 240 metres. They were said to be the 'greatest number of distinct and independent dune systems anywhere in the world' in the final report of the Fraser Island Environmental Enquiry, a detailed study which led to the Australian Government banning the export of minerals, so saving the island from

destructive change by mining companies.

Lakes have been formed here—in a landscape completely made from sand, a material normally so porous that it allows water to penetrate and disappear. This can happen when humic material from dead plants collects with iron minerals in hollows among the dunes over long periods of time, and gradually creates a layer that can hold water. Such lakes are said to be perched. There are over forty of them on Fraser Island, many large and very beautiful. Lake Boemingen, 200 hectares in area, is claimed to be the largest perched lake in the world.

In some of the lakes the water is so clear that you may step in without being aware that you are not on dry land. In others the water is a rich red from dissolved humic material and has the peaty look common in swampy places.

This is only the visible freshwater and huge amounts are held in a great dome deep in the sand. This liquid floats on the more dense saltwater of the sea and steadily flows through lakes or creeks, or straight into the ocean.

In a land as arid as Australia this immense quantity of freshwater is a 'mineral' resource of great value, often

Left and right (top and bottom):
The hardy Pandanus tree grows well around the sandstone cliffs on Fraser Island.

Below:
Fraser Island is the largest sand island in the world. Rain percolating through the sand leaches out minerals and deposits them again. These ironstone concretions make an interesting pattern in an area named Rainbow Gorge.

Over (pp. 64–5):
Sand extending for as far as the eye can see on Fraser Island, one of the Great Sandy Islands.

Above and right:
The sand mass of Fraser Island would not seem
capable of holding water, but over many years the
remains of plants and minerals have gradually lined
the hollow with an impervious layer and they are
called perched lakes. Lake Boemingen is probably
the largest such perched lake in the world.

Above:
The peculiarity of rainforest growing on what is almost pure silica has amazed botanists as plants cannot survive on sand and water alone. This rainforest is at Central Station on Fraser Island.

overlooked, or, at best, underrated.

Plant habitats from tall rainforest to wet heaths are found on this sand surface. (In southeast Queensland wet heath is usually called *wallum*, the Aboriginal word for a banksia found in such places.) The peculiarity of rainforest growing on what is almost pure silica has amazed botanists as a plant cannot live on sand and water alone. This paradox has been explained by rainforest experts Dr L. J. Webb and Dr W. T. Williams in the following way:

Nutrients come in with the rain or are blown along by the wind, both from the mainland and from the sea. To these are added the materials of decayed plants, returned into the growing stages in a closed cycle. This can run forever unless a change in climate or man's activities break the cycle.

Bushfires may cause a loss of some minerals in certain areas as the ash in which they collect may be washed away into lower levels. These lower areas, however, are enriched and rainforest can grow there protected against further fire by the sand walls that surround them.

Dr Webb and Dr Williams write '. . . the most striking forests are those of Satinay *(Syncarpia hillii)*, a species found elsewhere only on the adjacent mainland at Cooloola; the tall, almost cylindrical stems soar to 180 feet (55 metres), and with their shaggy furrowed barks resemble a miniature Californian Redwood stand'.

They also point out that Fraser Island is a botanical junction between south and north.

On the eastern side a spectacular beach runs the length of the island and contains a 40 kilometre stretch of similar coloured sands to those that made Cooloola famous among tourists.

All the land-forming and land-destroying processes have made this island a natural laboratory for the study of the climates of the last million years and so of great value to climatologists. Change continues as sand drifting about half a

metre a year engulfs some of the lakes and forests. Sometimes this movement began when man destroyed the plant growth which previously firmly anchored the sand.

Cooloola

This huge sand mass can be considered as one of the 'islands' of the area, even though changing sea levels and moving sand has tied it once more to the mainland. Some 23,000 hectares of this magnificent area, including the western catchment of the Noosa River, has been reserved as a national park.

Like Fraser Island, it is not only the sand masses, but also the suite of wildlife that flourishes in this area of high rainfall, that attracts attention.

The coloured sands of Cooloola are outstanding. The dunes extend about 10 kilometres inland and rise to heights of 240 metres. They all belong to the same 'family' of which Fraser, Moreton and Stradbroke Islands are well-known members. They have a complex history, recent research indicating that the oldest dunes in the area were formed some 400,000 years ago. The sands of Rainbow Beach are thought to be the oldest of the systems, and the last coloured sands were formed within the last 10,000 years.

The colour is due to the coating of individual grains with iron and aluminium oxides, and varying mixtures produce the range of colours. When black sands are added to the others, nature has a

Right:
A green turtle with a heavy algal encrustation on its shell beached on Fraser Island. Usually turtles come ashore only when nesting, but occasionally one may sun itself in the shallows or be trapped by a falling tide.

Below:
Rainforest at Central Station, Fraser Island.

wonderfully varied palette to use in painting the dunes.

The coating also traps nutrients such as calcium, magnesium, potassium, phosphorus and sulphur. These riches are absorbed by dune fungi that bring them into the plant cycle where small shrubs, taller plants, and finally towering giants of the forest can use them.

Such fungal partners are particularly important in rainforests. A finger stroked through the litter of the forest floor will reveal hundreds of white threads called *hyphae*—the feeding parts of the fungi. Co-operation between many kinds of plants is the base on which rainforest empires are built!

In similar fashion to Fraser Island the mass of sand dunes is one vast water reservoir. Measurements show that some 360,000 cubic metres of water go into the sand each year resulting in 9,000 million cubic metres being held in store. It has been suggested that this amount of water would be enough for the needs of a city of 150,000 people and that too greedy a grab for one natural resource may mean an even more important resource is lost.

For most Australians the beauty of Rainbow Beach with its backdrop of wildlife and forests is treasure enough and should be kept for all time.

LAMINGTON NATIONAL PARK

This is a legendary place for Queenslanders as here was born the State national park movement and the individuals involved are a roll call of honourable names.

Just as the beauty of the country south

Below and top left:
Rainbow Beach, part of the Cooloola coloured sands, that stretch about 10 kilometres and rise to heights of 240 metres. The colour is due to grains of sand being coated with a mixture of iron and aluminium oxides.

of Sydney encouraged New South Wales to declare the first national park in Australia in 1879 (only seven years after the world's first such reserve was dedicated in the United States) the grandeur of the mountains southwest of Brisbane stirred local naturalists into action.

The hills of the region, clothed in dense green vegetation, can be seen from the high towers of the city stretching in a great arc of about 300 kilometres with the Macpherson and Great Dividing Ranges as the backbone.

The wealth of rainforest and wet eucalypt forest led an early naturalist to exclaim that while Sydney had its magnificent blue mountains as a backdrop to their city, Brisbane had its green mountains as an equally fascinating hinterland.

Today the name Green Mountains is used by most visitors for an area that is more prosaically, and with little justification, officially called Lamington National Park.

The backbone rocks of the area were formed by the outpouring of the Tweed Shield Volcano whose core is Mount Warning. From these fiery vents poured floods of basalt. These volcanic rocks, eroded over millions of years, created an escarpment 1,100 metres above sea level which today is part of the Scenic Rim reserve.

Bordering New South Wales and Queensland it is high country with 25 peaks above 1,000 metres and a wealth of plant and animal life.

The first steps in the preservation of these gorges began in 1878 when Robert Collins, then President of the Royal

Below right:
Antarctic Beech forest in the Lamington National Park.

Bottom:
The Elebana Falls in the Lamington National Park, part of the Scenic Rim.

Geographical Society of Queensland, urged the setting aside of particular areas. He died in 1913 possibly unaware that his pioneering efforts had not been wasted.

The next person to work for the gorge's preservation was the son of a sawmilling family, young Romeo Lahey, who first visited the mountains in 1908. Conservation societies of the time gave him strong support, but it was his background in a milling family and his tireless canvassing of local opinion to back his dream that finally convinced the government that a national park should be dedicated.

It was at this point that the O'Reilly family came into the story. Pioneer settlers, they came to this country in the never-ending search for farmland which animated so many Australians. They left the Blue Mountains of New South Wales for the newly opened up Green Mountains and fell in love with their beauty.

One of the sons, Bernard O'Reilly, who was a keen amateur naturalist, later became the first ranger in the park. His family set up a guesthouse at one end of the reserve and from here Bernard made his long and arduous search for a crashed Stinson plane in 1937.

He saved the lives of the two survivors, telling the dramatic story in his book *Green Mountains*, a story not only about heroism but also of his abiding love of the bush.

At the other end of the park another well-known Australian, Arthur Groom, set up a guesthouse called Binna Burra and few visitors to Lamington have not stayed at both places.

The history of preservation in this mountain area did not end with the dedication of the national park. Another forester and sawmiller, John Lever, worked hard in the first campaign and in 1973 became alarmed at the destruction of nearby forests. He helped form the Border Ranges Preservation Society.

Their interest spread to nearby New South Wales where the battle to save the rainforests was also a struggle to create national parks which would link with those in southeast Queensland.

The old dream of a Scenic Rim Reserve came to life. The first step came with the reservation of Cunninghams Gap National Park in 1909, then Lamington. Finally, in 1977, the Queensland Government accepted the Rim concept and started to set aside a chain of reserves to turn the hundred-year-old dream into a reality.

South of the border the New South Wales Government decided in 1982 to protect all the remaining rainforests, setting most aside in secure reserves. So the green mountains with their inset jewels of rainforests will delight visitors for generations to come on both sides of the border.

Many books have been written about the scientific as well as the aesthetic interest of rainforest around the world. Here is a habitat where forest is piled on forest, until the plants can grow no taller. Layers of trees at about 20, 40 and 60 metres are most common and it is the final roof of leaves that reduces the sunlight to negligible proportions. The forest floor is so dimly lit that it is almost devoid of plant growth, except for those few species which can survive with a minimum of energy. These kinds of plants are the ones that flourish as pot plants in the dim light of homes and offices, reminding people of the lush, green world of the rainforest. Fortunately in all the eastern States rainforests survive close to capital cities and are easily visited.

Along the northern and eastern coasts there are a number of different kinds of rainforest. Some have in their higher areas a grouping called Antarctic Beech forest. These southern beeches flourished in the old days of Gondwanaland when the southern continents were linked in one huge landmass. Evidence for that ancient alliance is shown by the number of plants and animals they share—among them the southern beeches. Today they are found only in South America, New Zealand, Tasmania, some eastern mainland states, New Caledonia and New Guinea.

A walk through a beech wood is entrancing. The vast boles often show where an earlier giant grew and are covered with moss and ferns: epiphytes that cling without harming their host.

Wherever you walk in Lamington National Park you can hear the voice of the bush. Five hundred waterfalls provide water music while the rush of wind in the treetops during summer showers explains why it is known to Brisbane residents as the birthplace of summer thunderstorms.

Some 140 kilometres of well-organised walking tracks means that the pressure of

The Morning Glory is a cloud mass that rolls across the shallow waters of the Gulf of Carpenteria.

the visitors does not create the environmental problem of a beauty spot being 'loved to death'. Good management has kept intact all the old beauty.

Looking south over the valleys from Mount Bithongabel you can still capture something of the feeling of those earlier naturalists who camped near here in December 1918 and did their part in drawing public attention 'to the scientific and scenic value of this great national park'.

Their story is told on a monument in the forest nearby but the best memorial to

increasingly interested in this strange cloud and from their studies it seems that while there is no rain with the Morning Glory, there may be mist. As it passes over a weather station, there is always a pressure jump on recording instruments and often a drop in the humidity. Sometimes wind squalls may accompany it.

It rolls along between 8 and 15 kilometres per hour although some observers claim it can move faster. The normal one roll of a Morning Glory cloud is spectacular enough, but at times there may be up to eight successive rolls.

Not all are seen over the sea. In the magazine *Overlander*, outback writer Dick Eussen described his experience near the Gregory River near Burketown, where spectacular Morning Glory clouds may be seen. 'Majestic and awesome, it could be likened to a horizontal tornado as the roll advanced . . . The sun vanished behind the cloud and an eerie light radiated about us as the first roll swept over . . .'

Not all travellers will be fortunate enough to see a Morning Glory. It took Dick Eussen sixteen years to get a good photograph.

Recent research has found that these solitary waves are widespread and in a study carried out over a six year period near Tennant Creek more than 1,000 were recorded. Most cannot be seen and are detected by barographs and some have been tracked for hundreds of kilometres.

those who worked so hard to preserve this beauty for future generations is Lamington itself and the associated national parks collectively called The Scenic Rim.

THE MORNING GLORY

Most of us are familiar with the creeper that given sun and rain will gradually overwhelm a garden, but there is another Morning Glory known to those who live near the Gulf of Carpentaria.

Outback dwellers pride themselves on their ability to read the clouds that indicate stormy or fine weather. Yet not all movement in the air is visible; there are invisible and puzzling 'solitary waves',

which were recorded scientifically as far back as 1834. These solitary waves can cause a disaster when a plane flies into a wall of moving air in what appears to be a clear sky.

At times the solitary waves become visible, as in the case of the Morning Glory, a cloud mass that rolls across the shallow waters of the Gulf of Carpentaria. The long cigar-shaped mass of horizontal cloud can extend for more than 100 kilometres and usually appears before dawn, although it can be seen between 2 am and 8 am. It is often as low as 40 metres above the water, may be between 100 and 250 metres thick, and in the early morning sun may vary from inky black to blue in colour.

Meteorologists have become

WALLAMAN FALLS

Why is it that people flock to waterfalls? Even the smallest of cascades delights while the largest, like Niagara Falls in north America and Victoria Falls in central Africa, are among the world's great tourist attractions.

A waterfall is usually created in the young stages of the life of a river as it cuts into its bed with all the force produced by water running over a steep slope. It often begins when a resistant rock layer overlies softer, more easily eroded rock. Then the swirl as the water hits the bottom and bounces on pebbles creates a pothole that eats back into the waterfall base.

In time the overhang becomes too great and the weight cracks off the tougher upper layer and the waterfall retreats. Such a recession can be rapid—Niagara Falls is moving back along the river flow at the rate of a metre a year.

Australia is not richly supplied with waterfalls of world-class standard, but surprisingly we have two among the world's highest in terms of sheer drop, although not in the volume of tumbling water. New South Wales leads in numbers of permanent falls having thirty-two of them with a drop of more than 60 metres. One, at Wollomombi, has a first drop of 335 metres with several smaller falls that make a grand total of 481 metres.

Queensland has seventeen permanent falls of more than 60 metres. Of these, the greatest is at Wallaman near Ingham, with a drop of 280 metres and an additional fall of 70, making a total of 350 metres.

Wallaman has the additional advantage of a good road going to near its summit, which has a magnificent view of the surrounding rainforest.

In season the mass of white water and filmy spray at its base is framed with umbrella tree flowers, and gauzy circles of rainbow add to its splendour.

CHANNEL COUNTRY

And I saw the vision splendid
Of the sunlit plains extended
And at night the wondrous glory
of the everlasting stars.

Many places in Australia would fit this poem's imagery, the Channel Country as well as any. At the time the poem was written, however, only birds could have had the greatest view of all, which is an aerial view of the Channel Country flooded. Then as far as the eye can see is a vast circle, crossed with hundreds of meandering ribbons of water edged with dark-green trees while the grass is as vivid a green as ever covered the fields of far-off Ireland.

This enormous section of southwest Queensland is covered with rich alluvial soil brought down by millennia of floods from the headwaters of the major rivers of this arid country. These are the tributaries of the Lake Eyre drainage system, in particular the Cooper, the Diamantina and the Georgina, all romantic names in a romantic countryside.

The Aboriginals once lived well here, roaming along the river flats in the dry times and spreading out widely every two years or so when the rivers broke their banks and spread over the plains. For up to 50 kilometres the land became a sea of muddy water and then in a few months, a sea of grass.

The plants that nourished hordes of wallabies and kangaroos, as well as bustards and other plant-eating birds, became the target of white squatters. Flocks of sheep and herds of cattle spread over the plains, for the pastures here include the highly valued Mitchell grass.

Along the flats also grow Cooper clover, channel millet and bluebush, with saltbush on the more saline areas.

This area attracted the most daring of all Australian outlaws, Captain Starlight. He and his gang rounded up 1,000 head of cattle in yards they built in a corner of a huge station property, then drove them south to ready markets in South Australia.

This incredible feat, not only of robbery but also of horsemanship, captured the public's imagination and led to the writing of the early classic, *Robbery under Arms*. In his book Rolf Boldrewood wove into a tapestry of half truth and half fiction, a story not only about cattle stealing, but also about the rich, exciting life of the early gold rush, with the ever-fascinating Australian bush as a background.

Because of the flatness of the Channel Country—it has a gradient of only about 1 in 5,000—when the rivers flow they meander in vast arcs across the grey and black soil plains to fill huge lakes that often remain after the floods. Some of these semi-permanent lakes are 30 kilometres long and 12 metres deep.

The main tree of the region is the coolibah, which is an ideal wood for campfires. Natural levees humped along the water channels assist in the creation of deeper pools that are feeding grounds for fish and waterfowl as well as mammals such as the long-haired rat. In good years these rodents breed to plague proportions and devour everything in their path.

With the persistence of lemmings some even manage to swim across the great width of Lake Eyre when it is full, only to die of starvation on the arid southern shores.

The plants on which all these animals live include nardoo, the fern that grows outback in shallow water flats, and the sesbania pea whose flowers brighten the grey-green landscape. Other tussock grasses and shrubs grow over most of the flood plain and the woodlands are formed by coolibahs.

Deep-red desert dunes, clothed with spinifex and other desert-loving plants, eremophilas, mulga, bloodwoods and grevilleas, push through the Channel Country alluvials like long fingers.

Mitchell grass, the wonder pasture of so much of northern Australia that nourished the vast herds of the cattle kings, grows on the grey clay soils. Even so, one of the early pastoralists was to grimly exclaim that although they might be kings, their castles could be blown away on a puff of wind when the long droughts withered away the plant life.

REMNANTS OF VOLCANOES

Immense volcanic activity occurred long ago, in the period geologists call the lower Cainozoic era, in the eastern areas of Queensland and in northeast New South Wales.

Right:
Wallaman Falls has the second longest drop of any waterfall in Australia. The water plunges in two leaps, the first of 280 metres, the second of 70, making a total fall of 350 metres.

Over (pp. 76–7):
Mt Warning in northeast New South Wales is the volcanic remnant of the heart of a giant volcano.

Mount Warning is a present-day remnant of a time of dramatic outpourings of molten lava into the surrounding country. Such spectacular landforms are called shield volcanoes and good examples are in the Hawaiian Islands, Mauna Loa being the best known as well as the highest.

The central craters of such shield volcanoes are huge areas, with pit craters once filled with lakes of molten lava. The highly fluid basalts flow readily and in the case of the Mount Warning eruption the cooled rock created many well-known ranges, such as Main Range and the Bunya Mountains to the north. The upper layers of the basalts formed in those far-off times still keep their almost horizontal bedding, with a gentle slope away from the volcanic centre from which they poured.

Queensland had other centres in the southeast. The Glasshouse Mountains, made from less fluid rocks than basalt today, remain as plugs, necks, stocks and dykes along a north-south zone that runs for 80 kilometres north of Caboolture. These landforms are made of rocks called trachytes.

Glasshouse Mountains

This exotic name conjures up visions of steep slopes glittering like glass, but nothing could be further from reality. The Glasshouse Mountains, being the plugs of volcanoes which dominated this region some 25 million years ago, are made of a dark-grey, volcanic material.

As the vents cooled the last of the molten material hardened to form plugs or stocks. Being more resistant to erosion than the ash and other material spewed out by the eruptions, they remain to this day rearing skyward some 550 metres above the flatter country around them. Their forms vary from needle-shaped spires to massive, although steep-sided, domes.

As Captain James Cook sailed past the shoreline from where they can be seen their vertical shape brought back memories of his homeland and he wrote, 'These hills lie but a little way inland, and not far from each other; they are remarkable for the singular form of their elevation which very much resembles a glasshouse and for which reason I called them the Glass Houses.'

Cook was speaking of the furnaces of industrial England, not fairy-like glittering palaces.

The mountains were important reminders of the Dreamtime for the local Aboriginals and we use their names for them: Mount Beerwah ('up in the sky') is 556 metres high, Mount Coonowrin is 532 metres, Mount Tibrogarga ('squirrel eater'—the gliding marsupial still common in the forest country of eastern and

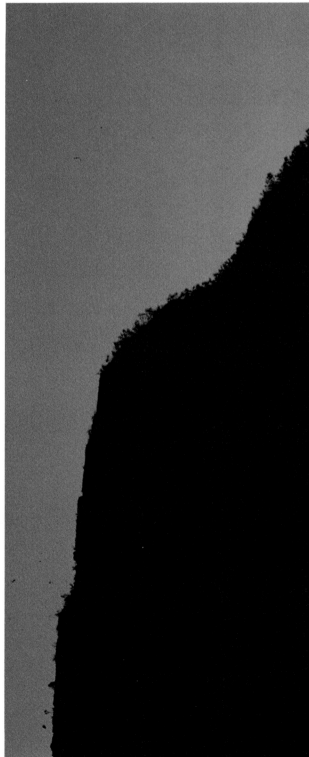

Right and far right:
Erosion often leaves remnants of volcanic eruptions in a variety of strange shapes. These mountains north of Caboolture are the remains of volcanic plugs and other lava flows, that looked to Captain Cook like the 'glass houses' or furnaces of industrial England.

78

northern Australia) is 393 metres, while Mount Ngungun ('charcoal'—an apt description of its sombre rocks) is the lowest at 236 metres.

Mount Coonowrin, although not the highest, is the most dramatic with smooth, sheer sides.

Viewed from the high country to the north, this assemblage of ancient volcanoes is a remarkable sight in a State noted for its landscapes.

THE CARNARVONS

'Our admiration of the valley increased at every step. High sandstone rocks fissured and broken like pillars and walls and the high gates of the ruined castles of Germany, rise from the broad sandy summits of many hills on both sides of the valley . . .' wrote the German explorer, Ludwig Leichhardt, of the central highlands of Queensland.

His second in command and companion, English explorer John Gilbert, thought in more British terms: 'These curious rocks present a most singular appearance, and are the more striking from being on the tops of high ridges. They resemble, when seen from a distance, ruins of old castles and Druidical stones . . .'

For the Aboriginals, who found this maze of hills and valleys good hunting grounds, every part would have had its creation story in the legends of the Dreamtime.

The central highlands is often called the Roof of Queensland, which is an apt title. Being the watershed of a number of rivers flowing in all directions it has also earned the name 'Home of the Rivers'.

It is not only the home of present-day rivers, but also the starting place for an underground mass of water that slowly flows westward—the Great Artesian Basin whose intake beds outcrop here.

The important geological history of the region began some 200 million years ago when sediments were being deposited in an area of subsidence today called the Bowen Basin. This complex of sedimentary and volcanic rocks contains important coal seams and sandstones that are the reservoirs of oil and gas.

The first layers of sand deposited in this ancient sea are today a coarse brown sandstone found to the east of the main camping area of the Carnarvon Gorge National Park. Then came a layer of clay and mud which later changed to shales, a close-packed impervious layer.

On top of these muds were immense deposits of sand and other materials which together make up the 4,000 metre thick rocks of today. The best known of these is called Precipice Sandstone. A beautiful white rock, it provides most of the spectacular scenery in the park. It was also an ideal painting surface for the Aboriginals who found the overhangs and deeper caves offered shelter from the cold and wet of winter.

Although originally a sediment this rock does not show obvious layering. Its lines of weakness are widely spaced vertical joints which allow weathering and the falling away of great blocks to the valley, leaving behind sheer cliffs. The jointing enabled the weird forms that early explorers likened to castles and stone-age memorials to be sculpted by rain, wind and running water.

The Precipice Sandstone is one of the important aquifers of the Great Artesian Basin. Rainwater flows along the joint lines until it is held by the shale formation below.

Above the sandstone is a capping of basalt. All these steps in geological time can be studied while climbing from the floor of the gorge where the creek runs over the shales. After the stiff climb up the Precipice Sandstone, and two more sandstones of the artesian basin, the basalt capping layer is reached at the top of the gorge.

This variety of underlying rocks weathers to a variety of soils which nourish a variety of plants growing on the surface, and it follows that a fascinating assortment of wildlife is available for study in this 30,000 square kilometre area.

The most popular walk is along the Carnarvon Gorge, which runs for 30 kilometres with walls up to 200 metres high. At times the walls come within 50 metres of each other, although they are usually about 400 metres apart.

Near the campsite forest giants such as white-barked flooded gum, spotted gum, and swamp mahogany tower above the river sheoaks, drooping bottlebrush and native cherry. Cycads line the walking paths, many of which are probably hundreds, if not thousands of years old.

Side tracks reveal even more striking plant species. In one narrow cleft magnificent examples of king ferns grow. This giant among ferns with a massive trunk that may be as much as a metre in diameter is found throughout Queensland. In this gorge the ferns, thought to be the world's largest species with their 5 metre long fronds, form a small forest.

In sheltered places are fairy dells covered with mosses, tree ferns, king orchids, figs and a wealth of other plants.

With the vegetation so diverse, so too are the animals. Friendly grey kangaroos forage around the tents for titbits, the shy, pretty-faced wallabies come in at dusk for their share, and the pied currawongs ransack bags for hidden food. At night

Above:
A moss garden pool at Carnarvon Gorge.

Left:
The main walking track, originally made by cattle, in the main gorge at Carnarvon Gorge.

brushtail possums scavenge the camp tables while high overhead gliders tap the sap of trees or sip nectar from flowers in a steady and often noisy search. You may see their dark shapes as they glide from tree to tree. Sometimes they are joined by those much more skilled aerial dwellers, the fruit bats, who are equally avid for nectar and blossom and enjoy soft fruits as a bonus.

The Aboriginals came into this treasure house of nature thousands of years ago. A great deal of archaeological research has been carried out, particularly in the Carnarvon Gorge area where some fifty sites have been studied.

The most obvious and attractive of such sites are those where the Aboriginals decorated the soft white walls with their art. Stencils make up about 55 per cent of the paintings in the two largest sites: the Art Gallery and Cathedral Caves. Engravings make up 4 per cent and freehand painting makes up only 2 per cent of the galleries.

The freehand paintings and engravings are not easy to interpret, except in a few cases, but the stencils are obviously the result of parts of the human body, or weapons, being held against the wall and sprayed with ochre paint so that an image is left behind.

Through centuries of Aboriginal occupation the floors of the caves have become important archaeological stores of information. Rubbish, whether ancient or modern, tells a great deal about a culture. Studies in the Cathedral Cave, first excavated in 1975 by archaeologist J. M. Beaton, showed that this shelter was first used about 3,500 years ago.

It was not a regular campsite, being mainly used for the making of stone tools. The 454 implements and 5,000 chips found give some idea of its quality. A variety of bone tools have also been found and these, with fragments of the bone left behind after meals, shed light on the animals hunted in the area, which range from catfish, lizards and snakes to a number of marsupials.

Plant remains do not last well so it is not surprising that only one empty shell of the local cycad has been found, although such plant food would probably have provided at least 70 per cent of the food supply.

The large number of cycads in the valley, the permanent waterholes, and the

Aboriginal art and midden remains are strong evidence that this would have been an important ceremonial site. Easily obtained food was an essential requirement when Aboriginals gathered for ceremonies that often took days, weeks or even months to complete.

Dr Beaton comments that it is a puzzle why, with all these advantages, the Cathedral Cave was used only 3,500 years ago, instead of much earlier, as about 35 kilometres to the northwest an earlier dig showed that the Aboriginals were in the area 19,000 years ago. He suggests that large ceremonies perhaps appeared only fairly recently in Aboriginal history!

The more ancient occupation was at Kenniff Cave, named in honour of two brothers who were as notorious in Queensland as the Kelly gang were in Victoria, and for the same reason.

So, from the first people in Australia, through the explorers, bushrangers and first white settlers to the modern tourists, this Roof of Queensland has been a mecca. Its wilderness now contains mines, farmlands and forests, as well as excellent bushwalking and camping, so the whole area needs the most careful management to retain its economic, as well as its recreational, values.

As it is also the Home of the Rivers its importance as a water catchment in safeguarding the quantity and quality of the water flowing to the farmlands on the plains is enough to ensure the greatest care.

Fortunately a number of national parks have already been set aside—Carnarvon Gorge at 217,000 hectares is the largest, while Isla and Robinson Gorges lie to the east. Conservationists also hope that a chain of national parks and State forests will be created across the central highlands.

LAWN HILL GORGE

The almost unknown Lawn Hill Gorge takes its unusual name from the station property which encompasses it on the western border of Queensland.

The main gorge comes as a surprise to the visitor driving on a rough bush track across creeks and low hills. Cadjeputs line the permanent waterholes and pandanus provides an exotic fringe, while in the low shrubbery along the water's edge the rare

purple-crowned wren flaunts its almost unbelievable royal plumage; or at least the male does while the female skips ahead in sombre brown.

These gorges, eroded in sandstone country, are best enjoyed by boat with an occasional landing to climb to a high point and enjoy the full beauty of the landscape spreading to the horizon.

Aboriginals apparently found it an ideal place 30,000 years ago and old heaps of charcoal show where they once camped to hunt the streams for freshwater fish and the long-clawed freshwater crayfish, today a delicacy for knowledgeable visitors.

At the main camping spot is the famous Painted Pool where floodwaters have etched the sandstone walls into a suite of colours that glow even more richly at sunrise and sunset. At the head of this gorge are small waterfalls fringed with ferns.

To the west of the sandstone gorges are areas of limestone with other gorges where the dissolving of surface rock by acid rainwater created a pattern of crevices called grikes.

Local enthusiasts claim that here is a potential reserve the equal of Kakadu in the Northern Territory. Naturalist Jim Gasteen, who has made a major survey of the area, has recommended that the present tiny reserve of a few thousand hectares be expanded a hundredfold, and the State government has announced plans for a national park in the area.

Right:
A little-known area of mid-western Queensland, Lawn Hill, has recently been made into a national park. Rivalling Katherine Gorge in beauty and interest, it will become a tourist haven.

Northern Territory

KAKADU NATIONAL PARK

Above:
An aerial view of the floodplains at Kakadu National Park, with the escarpment in the distance.

Left:
The floodplains of the South Alligator River in Kakadu National Park.

Nearing the end of his long journey from southern Queensland the explorer Ludwig Leichhardt came into the country we now call Kakadu, '. . . Suddenly the extensive view of a magnificent valley opened before us. We stood with our whole train on the brink of deep precipice, of perhaps 1,800 feet descent, which seemed to extend far to the eastward. A large river, joined by tributary creeks coming from east, south-west and west, meandered through the valley.'

Travelling across the vast plains a few days later, he wrote, '. . . not a night had passed without long files and phalanxes of geese taking their flight up and down the river, and they often passed so low that the heavy flapping of their wings was distinctly heard . . . No part of this country we had passed, was so well provided with game as this . . . The cackling of geese, the quacking of ducks, the sonorous note of the native companion, and the noises of black and white cockatoos, and a great variety of other birds, gave to the country, both day and night, an extraordinary appearance of animation . . .'

This region had nourished a large population of Aboriginals for tens of thousands of years but Leichhardt did not have the time to study in any detail the art they had painted during their long stay.

Because of the richness of its wildlife, the beauty of its landscape, and the extent and diversity of its Aboriginal art galleries, the national park in this area was nominated and accepted for the World Heritage List.

The origins of this remarkable landscape are lost in the mists of a thousand million years. This section of Australia was a subsiding area, a huge basin into which sediments poured from the highlands to create new rocks, kilometres in thickness. Then the land rose and today forms the escarpment country, a deeply dissected sandstone plateau region. Here also are quartzites and conglomerates, and occasional streams follow the weakness of the many joint lines.

Much of this plateau is bare rock or has only thin soils that carry spinifex and stunted shrubs, but in the many deep valleys there are eucalypt forests as well as rainforests, relics of vegetation growing over much of the floodplains in past eras when rainfall was heavier.

The plateau meets the plains in the dramatic escarpment country, a 600 kilometre long zone. Here there are waterfalls such as Djim Djim and Twin Falls, with many intruding gorges, caves with cascades, and overhangs making ideal sites for cave paintings. Rock pools remain the year round and provide watering points during the dry season.

There is some argument as to exactly where Leichhardt saw his 'extensive view' and brought his men and horses down the escarpment as heights of 250 metres make ascent or descent difficult. The official opinion is that he came down into Deaf Adder Gorge, although some think it may have been along the slope near Djim Djim Falls. It would have been a precarious passage wherever it was.

The rocky slopes are the home of black euro, rock wallabies, rock possums, northern quolls and other marsupials, as well as native rodents and bats.

The sandstone plateau and escarpment has remained relatively unchanged since the coming of man, although the plains at the foot of the escarpment are very different today from what they would have been when the Aboriginals first settled the area.

It seems probable that man came here when the sea levels were at their lowest some 55,000 years ago. That was the time of a major ice age and the sea journey between Australia and the islands to the north was reduced to as short as some 50 kilometres.

During that period fires on the mainland would have been visible to people on the islands to the north, a certain indication to those watchers that a voyage to the south might bring them to an inhabited country suitable for settlement.

The land of Kakadu may have been colder and drier in those times but all the present habitats would have been there, although the sea would have been further to the north. It is thought that 9,000 years ago the monsoon rainforests had reached their maximum area, a coverage which later retreated, probably because of the regular firing of the Aboriginals, a part of their traditional hunting pattern which continues to some extent today. A similar shrinking of the rainforest took place on the east coast of Australia.

Today the lowlands are an area of undulating plains, although some ridges and hills break the uniformity. The plants vary a great deal but woodland and closer-packed forests dominate with pockets of rainforest growing where the lowlands meet the flood plains.

During the summer wet (which has an average of 1300 millimetres of rainfall) the great rivers and their many creeks break their banks and spread into huge sheets of water. Paperbark trees grow in the areas which are always wet, swamp vegetation dominates where the water remains between 6 and 9 months, while in the areas underwater from 2 to 6 months sedges are the major plant group.

On this plantlife a variety of animals either feed or hunt the plant-eaters. Myriads of ducks and magpie geese, jabirus and brolgas, herons, and other wading birds live here; lily trotters move daintily over floating leaves and saltwater crocodiles alert for prey lurk below the surface.

Between the lowlands and the sea are the tidal flats where great rivers, the East and South Alligator and their associated tributaries, pour their sediments to form levee banks. Here the saltwater from the sea mixes with the freshwater of the rivers, the marine invasion penetrating more than a 100 kilometres from the ocean.

All these regions, interweaving with each other, produce a variety of habitats and species, including 960 kinds of plants, 273 birds, 51 native mammals, and 22

Above:
Cormorant and heron birds showing feather staining from the waters of a lagoon in Kakadu National Park.

Right:
Obiri Rock, an area of outstanding Aboriginal cave paintings, is one of the major attractions of Kakadu National Park.

frogs have already been identified in the 6,000 square kilometres of Kakadu National Park. This is the first stage of a reserve which it is hoped will one day extend westward to take in the Wildman River region.

The water buffalo was an unwise introduction that proved a disaster to the wildlife. Brought in between 1827 and 1849 as a food animal for a white garrison, it soon became feral and spread over the flood plains, finding the conditions ideal.

Their spectacular increase in numbers meant natural levee banks were broken and saltwater invaded freshwater swamps, destroying the plants and their associated animals. Overgrazing prevented the regrowth of trees and trampling feet caused havoc among ground-nesting birds, such as the scrubfowl, and destroyed the ground plants.

The menace of the feral pig which rooted in the soil in search of plants was soon added to that of the water buffalo, and the water plants of the freshwater lagoons which created so much of the beauty of the flood plains almost disappeared.

Since the formation of the national park, the numbers of both buffaloes and pigs have been reduced and the natural history interest has begun to return. The change in the most popular areas during the last ten years verges on the miraculous.

Twenty years ago the plains were desolate wastelands in the dry season with great herds of wandering buffaloes. The pools were devoid of lilies and other plants and poor in animal life. Today the muddy waters have become clear and the lagoons are alive with flowers and birdlife.

Above:
A ground goanna defies an enemy.

Left:
The Leichhardt grasshopper is a strikingly coloured insect, rediscovered some years ago after having not been recorded for 100 years.

Below:
Water plants decorate the pools of the Magela Plains.

Over (pp. 90–1):
Stately brolgas stalk in the shallow waters of Kakadu National Park.

Grass is beginning to cover the plains that once looked like ploughed fields and clumps of paperbarks and other trees are gradually re-establishing themselves.

In November 1978 the traditional owners of this rich landscape leased it to the Australian National Parks and Wildlife Service so that it could be kept for all time as part of Australia's heritage. One reason for this was the need for management that would repair the mistakes of the past and ensure that mining and other activities did the least harm.

It was symbolic that the proclamation of this park was one hundred years after the establishment of Royal National Park near Sydney, Australia's first park and the second in the world. Royal National Park, however, is a State park, unlike that at Yellowstone in the United States which is managed and owned nationally, as is Kakadu. Both Royal National Park and Kakadu are today controlled in such a way that the natural landscape values will be preserved for the future.

Kakadu is not only valued for its natural history. Its nomination for the World Heritage List stated that this region is 'outstanding on the basis of both its natural and cultural heritage'.

Within the park are areas of major archaeological interest. There are numerous archaeological sites, but these are not as interesting to the ordinary visitor as the many Aboriginal art galleries. These show a fascinating range of styles, including the dynamic drawings that show small human figures, often in elaborate costumes. Their weapons and the hunting methods shown suggest they were drawn when the sea was further to the north and Kakadu was a drier place than it is today.

Here too are the famous x-ray paintings, where as well as the animal's shape some of its internal organs are shown. Another famous art style is in the form of sticklike figures which are often heavily adorned. These figures are called 'Mimi' art and have their parallels in other parts of Australia and elsewhere in the world's prehistoric art forms.

It must be realised that while some of the paintings are old, many are modern, created during the last hundreds of years, yet they are in no sense primitive. Although the Australian Aboriginals lacked the sophisticated technology of the

Above:
Saltwater crocodiles, through many years of protection, are now becoming tame at Kakadu National Park.

Right:
Australia's only stork, the jabiru, seen against a skyline.

European world, in terms of their religion, dance, art, social structure and ability to cope with the environment they were completely modern, and their civilisation was similar to that of people's in other parts of the world. Indeed, it can be claimed that in their feeling for the country and the depth of their religious experience they excelled many European cultures. Proof of this richness of living is evidenced by these galleries, which in a sense are an historical picturebook.

Some of the paintings show hunters throwing spears as javelins without the aid of an implement we call a spear-thrower. This is evidence that they are at least 11,000 years old as the Tasmanian Aboriginals also lacked the spear-thrower and they were isolated from the mainland about that time. So the spear-thrower must have arrived here or been developed here, some time during the last 11,000 years. The Tasmanians had no boomerangs so the absence of this weapon is also some indication of the age of a particular gallery.

Some Aboriginal clans called these spear-throwers 'woomeras' and the space station in the South Australian desert country was given this name since it was a place where modern man threw 'javelins' into space.

The increase of fish in paintings in the galleries seems to indicate the gradual return of the sea and the development of extensive estuaries in the particular region. The appearance of blue, a hue missing from traditional paintings, shows that some Aboriginal artists, finding Reckitts washing blue in a white settler's house, decided to use a new material. Similarly, among the topics painted are Indonesian praus, guns, revolvers, and buffaloes. Even more modern paintings include aeroplanes and, although depicted in a strange way, the Sydney Harbour Bridge!

One of the management problems is how to keep the original quality of the drawings. The Kakadu sites are to some extent exposed to the weather, to the rubbing of animals against the rock walls, to damage caused by the mud homes of dauber wasps, and to other natural disfigurements.

In the past this did not matter as there was continual retouching by the Aboriginals carrying out their traditional rituals. At worst white settlement meant the death and disappearance of many of the tribal owners. Even when their numbers remained high, the loss of traditional beliefs through white contact often meant the end of Aboriginal interest in maintaining the galleries.

Should all conservation methods fail to slow the loss of this incredible collection of paintings, it may be necessary to encourage Aboriginal artists to keep their traditional skills so that they can carry on the retouching needed to keep the old quality alive.

One of the conditions of acceptance in the World Heritage List is that the nation which has ownership must do all in its power to keep the values for which the nomination was accepted.

The traditional owners have done their part by handing over control to the Australian government. They are also

playing their part in managing the area, by giving advice not only on the old ways of using the wildlife areas, but also on the art galleries and their conservation.

Some are being trained as rangers. From a visitor's point of view nothing could be more satisfying than to have a traditional owner of the land acting as a guide to its natural history and cultural wonders.

Keeping the quality can only be ensured by the continuing study of both plants and animals and how they interact so that all the present diversity can be retained.

Kakadu is unusual in world heritage listing in that it fulfils both the natural and cultural criteria for taking a place on this roll of honour. Its natural qualities are high: it has one-third of the known bird species of Australia, one-quarter of all the known freshwater fish, a plant component rich in species endemic to this region, a good population of the endangered saltwater crocodile, a wide range of habitats, and, finally, it is a major wetland in an arid continent.

To all this Aboriginal man has added at least 1,000 spectacular art galleries, and a large number of archaeological sites whose midden deposits will help provide information on the prehistoric economy of the region. Kakadu ranks high among the wonders of this continent.

'ISLAND MOUNTAINS' IN THE DESERT

Three 'island mountains' rise starkly out of a desert of red dunes south of Alice Springs. No other high land nearby takes away the impact of their solitary grandeur.

Ayers Rock is the best known of these island mountains, but the Olgas and Mount Connor are now regarded as part of the complex of landforms that has made this desert region famous.

From sunrise to sunset the changing angle of the light and the increase of dust in the air causes the three to vary in colour hour by hour. A mist of cloud and the colour changes yet again. At sunrise Ayers Rock may be pale reddish grey, then a break in the cloud gilds it for a moment.

When at sunset great crowds assemble on the lines of sandhills which ring the

rock it often glows a fiery red, the colour so often shown in tourist brochures. Stay-at-home viewers of colour transparencies of these three inselbergs, (which means island-mountains in German and is the geological name for them) can hardly believe anything can be so colourful, but the surprise is that it is all true!

Familiarity with these landforms does not diminish the visitor's feelings of awe and excitement, indeed the longer one stays near this natural grouping of rocks the deeper they become.

The rocks had their genesis more than 1,000 million years ago when a huge range of gneissic and granite rocks to the southwest were eroded and the spoil carried by rivers into a sea to the northwest.

As with all sediments, the texture varies, depending on the parent material and the distance from the shoreline. Some of the debris was coarse with boulders as large as a metre in size. These were later compressed into a rock called conglomerate, or, very appropriately, puddingstone.

This varied material has been surveyed to a depth of 6,000 metres, indicating how mountains can be worn away to ground level given enough time for the eroding forces of wind and water.

In the Ayers Rock region the pebbles became smaller and a sandstone called arkose was laid down. Arkose is a material in which erosion has been so rapid that the constituents of the parent rock have not been weathered completely. A close study of the surface of Ayers Rock reveals a variation of grain size, best seen with a hand lens but visible to the naked eye. In the Olgas the rocks vary from small pebbles to giant boulders several metres across. Mount Connor is built of an even-grained sandstone.

These three landforms are not boulders lying on the ground. Ayers Rock is not a giant pebble, a magnificent Devil's Marble. All three are tips of the one giant 'iceberg' of parent rock pushing its erosion residuals above the sea of sand around them.

The earth movements that lifted the sediments laid down in that sea of long ago left Mount Connor with its upper, more resistant, beds almost horizontal. Today it remains as a tent hill or mesa, the softer rocks below eroding away so that the upper blocks finally crack away

Above:
From the air Ayers Rock can be seen as sediments tipped by earth movements so they are now vertical. When first laid down under water millions of years ago they would have been horizontal.

Right:
From a distance Ayers Rock appears smooth. Nearer, a visitor can see where the ravages of time—erosion by rain, running water and wind—has weathered the rock.

Far right:
Ayers Rock is not a single giant pebble but the rounded tip of a mass of rock lying below the surface.

from the top and tumble down the slope.

Ayers Rock suffered the greatest movement and its beds of arkose sandstone became almost vertical, standing now at an angle of 70 degrees. They are easily recognisable as erosion has etched out the line of the old bedding planes. Because it is homogeneous, lacking the joints that normally fracture such a large mass, the weathering that has rounded its surface has worked in the process called spalling.

Flakes peel away from the main mass through moisture working into surface cracks. Rapid heating and cooling by the sun helps in breaking the outer skin allowing air and water to penetrate and begin their work. Such spalls can be very large and the 'kangaroo tail', on the northern face, is a massive example.

Strong winds ensure that little soil collects on the rock, except in some of the hollows on the top where shrubs and small trees flourish in good seasons.

Millions of years ago this rock appeared as an island in the middle of a large lake. Bores put down in a search for water passed through some 60 metres of sand and clay laid down in this ancient sea before they hit the parent arkose rock, proving the 'iceberg' shape of this inselberg.

West of Ayers Rock lie the Olgas. Here the bedding is more gentle, up to 30 degrees, and the whole mass is cut by joints at right angles. These lines of weakness have allowed erosion forces to cut the once-solid rock into many narrow valleys, breaking the once-solid mass into a group of domes. Mount Olga, rearing to 1,025 metres, is higher than Ayers Rock at 350 metres, and Mount Connor is slightly lower at 300 metres.

Dunes rise to nearly 20 metres in the nearby sand area and the soil serves as a giant sponge holding the rainwater. This is fortunate as the increasing number of visitors need adequate water supplies. Lake Amadeus, a 200 kilometre long mass of linked salt lakes and claypans, lies to the north. From the air it looks a carpet of shimmering beauty, enhancing the glories of the inselbergs to the south.

Today the thirty-six domes of the Olgas, 3,500 hectares in area and about 20 kilometres around, and Ayers Rock, 450 hectares and some 9 kilometres round, are part of a major national park of nearly 130,000 hectares. We hope Mount Connor will be included in the near future so that this residual can take its place in a triad of landforms which should be listed as a World Heritage area.

For tens of thousands of years the three red mountains have been part of an Aboriginal mythology that tied together the rocks, the desert and the surrounding countryside with its plants and animals, into a coherent, religious whole.

These island mountains had totemic importance, but in spite of their spectacular beauty the Aboriginals placed this area below other mythological centres in the desert in importance. For example, the western quoll centre, known to one group as Wapirka, was far more significant than Uluru (the Aboriginal name for Ayers Rock). An authority on the people of this part of the desert, Professor T. G. H. Strehlow, commented that a number of groups held part-shares in the traditions of Ayers Rock.

For Ayers Rock there were two main divisions. The southern aspect was associated with carpet-snake ancestors who battled with poisonous snake people. A major struggle took place at Mutilitjula, an important waterhole known to Europeans as Maggie Springs.

On the northern side, the mala or hare-wallaby people had a dramatic adventure as they moved across the sandhill country building their trapping fences. Shaped like a 'V' these were used to drive wallabies into an impasse where they could be killed by concealed hunters.

Disaster came in the form of a man-eating dingo that destroyed many of the people, despite the efforts of a kingfisher woman to rouse them from their sleep. Professor Strehlow translated the song-verses:

Loudly I scream—I the kingfisher:
My lungs are ready to burst with fear.

She tried to warn the mala men who were celebrating the successful wallaby hunt, dancing around a ceremonial hollow built near the waterhole:

With panting cries we are circling around,
Pushing our way through the thick night.

All these stories are written into the surface of Ayers Rock. To the Aboriginals it is a stone Bible where he who understands may read the story of creation.

Creation myths evolved with time. The non-poisonous carpet snakes, the venomous snakes, the mala and the kingfisher were there long before the coming of the black people, but the dingo arrived recently, possibly only a few thousand years ago and certainly during the last 10,000 years. So the dingo has been woven into the story, no doubt replacing a previous mythological carnivore.

It is tempting to speculate that the dingo replaced the marsupial lion or the Tasmanian tiger in Australian mythology, just as it appears to have replaced them in actuality. Many zoologists believe it was competition from the Aboriginal-introduced dingo which resulted in the tiger's extinction from the mainland during the last few thousand years, leaving it to survive only in Tasmania, where the dingo was stopped by the sea barrier of Bass Strait.

The Aboriginals themselves would also have kept a steady pressure on such carnivores, which would have been valued for their flesh and their teeth, which could be used as ornaments.

The first European explorer to see and name the Olgas was Ernest Giles. He only glimpsed Ayers Rock across the barrier of

Far right:
The climb up Ayers Rock.

Top, middle, far right and previous pp. 100–1:
The Olgas are made of coarser material than the sediments of Ayers Rock and the bedding is still horizontal, as it was when laid down in ancient lakes. Weathering has produced the rock patterns we see today.

Bottom:
The third of the three main rock formations of the Ayers Rock region is Mt Connor, a 5 kilometre long mass of quartzite. This photograph shows the ruins of the old Mt Connor Station in the foreground.

Lake Amadeus so it was W. A. Gosse who had the honour of naming it in 1873 after the State Premier Henry Ayers.

In doing so he described it as 'the most wonderful natural feature I have ever seen'. Giles, visiting it after Gosse, wrote, 'Mount Olga is the more wonderful and grotesque; Mount Ayers the more ancient and sublime'.

When at sunset we look west from Uluru to where the blue domes of the Olgas seem to be floating in a sea of red sand; or when we see Mount Connor rising like a red tent behind a glittering salt lake we can feel more clearly the kinship between humans and their environment; the feeling that earth, sky, plants and animals are all one.

FINKE RIVER AND PALM VALLEY

In its long journey to the Lake Eyre region the Finke River cuts through the James and Krichauff Ranges creating a series of fascinating gorges.

Ernest Giles named the Glen of Palms in 1872, writing that he was 'literally surrounded by fair flowers of ever-changing hue. The flowers alone would have induced me to name this "Glen Flora". But having found in it also so many of the stately palm trees I have called it "The Glen of Palms".'

The now much better known Palm Valley in a side creek of the Finke was missed by Giles as he continued north.

Top, right, far right and over (p. 106):
The palms of Palm Valley are related to the cabbage palms that grow in northern Australia and along the wetter east coast. They are relics of a period when the central region had better rainfall and today survive through their roots reaching the water under the dry river bed.

The palms, reasonably widespread in sheltered well-watered localities in this central desert, were a great surprise not only to Giles but also to scientists. These remnants, evidence that this was once a region of lush vegetation, survived the drying out central Australia suffered in the remote past.

These fan palms belong to the genus *Livistona* and are found in India, Southwest Asia and Australia, where they are common on the east coast. There is a southern patch of a few hectares in southeast Victoria and some grow in Western Australia at Millstream on the western end of the Hamersley Ranges. In northern Australia it forms forests and is one of the most common plants.

Another plant found in the region is sometimes called a 'palm' although it belongs to the cycads, a much more ancient group. Cycads evolved between ferns and plants with flowers, but so palm-like are the stiff leaves that they are used to decorate churches on Palm Sunday.

The cycads of the desert belong to the genus *Macrozamia* and in the southwest of Australia are called zamia palms. Their fruit, after treatment to remove the poison they contain, were an important source of carbohydrate for the Aboriginals.

The outer coating could be eaten raw, but the first white explorers, seeing these bright red delicacies lying about Aboriginal camps, suffered when they experimented with them as food. The sea captains, Cook and Fremantle, were both mildly poisoned by cycads.

During their thousands of years of occupation the Aboriginals had learnt how to treat them. They first crushed the nut and then washed out the poison.

Ferns and mosses grow in shaded pools in the valleys of the 50 kilometres of gorges cut into the sandstone here. The range of hard and soft rocks laid down in the seas of the Devonian age have now been etched into a variety of shapes by wind and water; and the government has set aside some 46,000 hectares of the valleys and gorges as national park to preserve the notable plantlife, desert animals and landforms of the Finke River region.

KINGS CANYON

The George Gill Range, a line of low hills running east and west and broken by a number of gorges, lies to the north of Ayers Rock. One of the gorges, Kings Canyon, has become a popular goal for visitors to the Centre.

A scientific party led by Baldwin Spencer explored the range in 1894 and was impressed with its wildlife. More recently, scientists from the Northern Territory Conservation Commission found it a treasure house of plants. Botanist Peter Latz called one valley 'a living plant museum' after it was discovered that of the 572 species recorded, sixty were rare and eight found nowhere else in central Australia.

A detailed survey of the western end of the George Gill Range may lead to a reserve being set aside to preserve this find.

It had long been an important place for the Aboriginals of the desert but Ernest Giles made the area known to the white settlers, naming the stream that runs out of one gorge Kings Creek in honour of one of his backers.

Exploring further he came to 'a high and precipitous wall of rock, under which was a splendid deep and pellucid basin of the purest water . . .'. Over this sheer cliff a waterfall tumbles after heavy rains.

It is possible to reach the top of the canyon by climbing the northeastern wall of the gorge entrance where a 'Garden of Eden' valley running at right angles to the gorge offers deep pools, sheltered by 30 metre high red walls. Palm-like cycads add to the bizarre beauty of the scene. A short distance from the top of the fall, Kings Canyon can be seen in all its beauty as it breaks through the red sandstone ranges.

The surface rocks of this range are a sandstone of Devonian age, laid down perhaps 400 million years ago. Ripple marks in many places in the rock sheets are mute evidence of the shallow waters that created these patterns in a soft sand bottom of the lake of long ago.

Uplift of these beds tilted them into the saucer shape geologists call a syncline, but the hollow is shallow so the beds are almost horizontal.

Vertical joints provide lines of weakness along which streams were able to cut the gorge. The prominent and dramatic face of the southeast wall is a joint plane where one side of the crack has fallen into the valley, to be carried away by the occasional streams.

On each side of the upper gorge erosional features, canyons, spires, boulders and a host of other forms have created a 'Lost City' landscape some visitors have described as being like the famous walled city of Zimbabwe. But it is no work of man; it is the work of nature tearing away the softer parts of the sandstone over millions of years.

The interest of the landforms is enhanced by the beauty of the plants:

Top and middle:
Kings Canyon is one of the landmarks of the Centre. The George Gill Ranges run east and west and are broken by a number of gorges—Kings Canyon is one of the most spectacular of them. After heavy rain the beauty of waterfalls is added to the rugged splendour of eroded sandstones. Palm-like cycads are an attraction of this area.

Bottom:
An aerial view of the landscape around Kings Canyon.

Above right:
This splendid member of the Dragon family was sighted at Kings Canyon.

snow-white ghost gums, grey-green mulgas and the 'funereal desert pines' as Giles so evocatively described them.

GOSSE BLUFF

One of the many dramatic landforms in central Australia, Gosse Bluff, is 4 kilometres in diameter and rises some 180 metres above the surrounding plain about 160 kilometres west of Alice Springs.

From the air it shows plainly as a crater with double walls, a natural 'pound'. The surface is bare compared with the surrounding desert, and small streams draw intricate patterns across the floor of the centre.

Some scientists think it is an astrobleme, or 'star wound', caused by a comet. A comet has a nucleus, perhaps 16 kilometres in diameter, of frozen water and gases, including ammonia, methane, carbon dioxide and carbon monoxide. This mixture makes up about 70 per cent of the material and the other 30 per cent. is a mass of other solids ranging from fine grains to large pieces of meteorites. The tail, streaming out for perhaps 160 million kilometres, is only a hazy cloud of material evaporated by the heat of the sun and elongated by the pressure of light.

The same scientists say that when a comet collides with the earth it could create a scar similar to that formed by a meteorite.

There are other suggested possibilities: that it is a meteorite whose remains have weathered away, or that in some kind of volcanic explosion gases exploded below the earth creating the vast saucer.

Certainly no meteoritic fragments have been found, but erosion over millions of years may explain the loss of much of the old structure. Also, holes drilled in a search for oil indicate that all impact details are shallow ones.

A further theory is that gases associated with ancient sediments may have violently pushed upwards, and, combined with water, thrown out the soil in all directions to create what is called a mud volcano. Such mud volcanoes, which have nothing to do with movements of lava, are common in oilfield areas.

So the creation of Gosse Bluff remains a mystery, with the weight of scientific opinion favouring an astrobleme, but whether from a meteorite or comet, is not yet proven. Yet there is growing scientific interest in collisions between the earth and material from outer space. For example, one of the great mysteries of our past is why many plants and animals, including the dinosaurs, apparently disappeared rather suddenly some 60 million years ago.

It has recently been discovered that the sediments of the boundary layer between these two epochs contain an over-abundance of iridium. It is thought this abundance may have been due to a massive visitor from space. A huge explosion could have shot masses of dust into the air which formed a world-wide, aerial blanket and cut off light from both land and sea.

Seven possible theories for the mass extinctions have been suggested, however, and the collision of earth and an object from outer space is only one of them.

Whatever its origins, Gosse Bluff remains one of the natural wonders of Australia, and a visual spectacle as well as a scientific mystery.

ORMISTON GORGE

This break in the ranges is justifiably called 'the opal of the centre'. Some of the cliffs that line the creek, which is a tributary of the much larger Finke River, rise 300 metres above the permanent waterholes whose shaded waters appear dark and mysterious.

The geology of the Gorge is complicated, but it has been carved out of the rocks by the work of running water eroding lines of weakness.

One of its features is The Pound, a natural amphitheatre drained by the creek. This enclosure is rarely seen as it lies at the end of a rough walking path along the creek bed strewn with boulders, but it is well worth a visit.

From wall to wall the enclosure is 10 kilometres across, with Mount Giles a major feature on the eastern side. In its passage from The Pound, Ormiston Creek creates a series of waterholes. The spectacle is enhanced by the colours of the rocky slopes which range from whites and yellows to rich browns and bright vermilions.

Right and below:
Gosse Bluff can be seen from the air as a huge basin or crater about 4 kilometres in diameter.

Rock called jasper, well known for its brilliance at the Western Australian river crossing at Marble Bar, is also found in this Pound and its banded formations add to the beauty of the area.

Ormiston Gorge may be the queen of these gaps in the ranges but others such as Glen Helen, Serpentine, Ellery to the west, Heavitree in the heart of Alice Springs, and Emily and Jessie Gaps to the east all have their beauty and natural history interest.

SIMPSONS GAP

Breaks in the ranges such as Simpsons Gap and Heavitree, and Emily and Jessie Gap, all result from an ancient river system, originally developed on a much more gentle slope but able to keep pace with a rising land by cutting deeper and deeper beds.

In these gorges a very resistant quartzite rock limited the sideways cutting and the resulting steep-sided walls provide the dramatic landforms we see today.

European man was able to appreciate only a few hundred years ago that such great gashes in the earth were made by running water carrying battering rams in the form of boulders, gravel and sand for millions of years. Until then they thought valleys were caused by earthquakes or mythological happenings.

So too did the Aboriginals. For them, Simpsons Gap was made by the totemic giant goanna, his path marked by many of the ghost gums that grow to the south of the cutting.

The visitor who walks along the sandy

Above:
Glen Helen Gorge, like Ormiston Gorge, has been cut through the quartzite rocks by eroding rivers. The stream that cut this spectacular channel is the Finke which, after breaking through these ranges, runs southeast to northern South Australia where it spreads over the plain. In good rainfall years the waters reach north Lake Eyre.

Left:
Ormiston Gorge lies on a tributary of the Finke River in the west MacDonnell Ranges. Its deep pools normally last through the dry years to be refilled in the wet.

bed of the river to the gap itself finds it hard to realise that a stream of water still flows below the dry surface, on a slow journey south to where it disappears into the dry lakes of the desert.

In Simpsons Gap the mass of rock is quartzite-weathered to a deep desert red and the walls show the lines of vertical joints. Brown schists, rocks of the ancient Arunta complex, believed to be about 2,000 million years old, can be seen on the eastern bank, south of the actual cut. River redgums line the bank and the walls of the gap glow red.

Towards late afternoon rock wallabies come out of their daytime shelters deep in rock crevices or overhangs. In these cooler and more humid retreats they avoid the water loss suffered by any desert creature exposed to the heat and drying air of the summer.

During the rare showers, which may come at any time of the year or on cool, overcast days the wallabies may be seen even at midday.

Because the surroundings of Simpsons Gap represent an excellent sample of the landforms of the MacDonnells as well as of the nearby desert plains, the original small reserve has now been extended. In these 30,000 hectares the naturalist can study the wildlife kept safe for all time in this national park.

THE MACDONNELL RANGES

In the heartland of Australia lie the MacDonnell Ranges, an intricate belt of mountains running east and west that is at first sight a barrier to travellers moving north or south.

A closer approach reveals a series of passes that provided the first white explorers with pathways through the hills. Today many of these 'gaps' have become famous landmarks.

The core of the ranges began with the laying down of rocks up to 2,000 million years ago. Part of the ancient western shield, they are mainly granites, gneisses and schists, and cover a much larger area than the MacDonnells. The great granite boulders of the Devils Marbles are part of the same formation. These rocks make up most of the northern flanks of the MacDonnells, but erosion over aeons of time has removed a great deal of material.

The seas and lakes of those times

received the erosion spoils to create new rocks and these, pushed up by earth movements, became the sandstones and other sediments which now make up the southern flank of the ranges.

At the same time the once-horizontal beds were folded into a series of anticlines (upward bending folds) and synclines (downward bending folds). These folds, containing rocks of differing hardness, were eroded at differing speeds and the 'grain' of the country began to show. When such a gently dipping rock is eroded to create long ridges with sharp edges, landforms called 'cuestas' form. They are found in many places, including Wilpena Pound, but are magnificently developed in these central Australian ranges.

At the height of mountain building the ranges rose to between 3,000 and 4,500 metres tall, but erosion has ground them to less impressive proportions. Mount Zeil at 1,511 metres and Mount Sonder at 1,334 metres are now the highest points.

Over the last 70 million years this region had a hot and humid climate and large lakes accumulated great beds of material. Some of them hold fossil crocodiles, kangaroos and the giant wombat-like diprotodon. It was at this time that the grey billy or silcrete and the iron-rich laterite formed to make the resistant capping of many of the hills.

Over the last million years the lush country slowly dried and the sand dunes of the Simpson reached the eastern flanks of the MacDonnells. Some of the old river systems, following the erosion lines laid down long ago, survived and today, although usually they are dry or only a series of deep pools, they can rise in flood and show something of their earlier glories.

It is interesting to compare this scientific story of creation with the legends of the Aboriginals who came to this area at least 40,000 years ago, possibly even earlier.

No man knew this world of legends as intimately as Professor T. G. H. Strehlow. He wrote of the time when for the Aboriginals this earth was a featureless plain with no sun, moon or stars. Then came the totemic ancestors. They could look like animals who thought and worked like humans, or like humans who could change into animals when the need arose.

Such heroes of the Dreamtime created every form in the landscape, plants and animals as well as the sun, moon and some of the stars. Often the most dramatic landforms to European eyes were only of minor significance to the Aboriginals but, he pointed out, '. . . the whole of Central Australia in a very real sense, was a sacred land for its original inhabitants'.

Professor Strehlow looked forward to the time when '. . . white Australians, too, may be able to look at Central Australia with new eyes; they will no longer see merely sandhills, ranges, boulders and waterholes, but will be able to share in those glimpses of its mythological past that once filled the hearts of the dark population with pride'.

KATHERINE GORGE

This beautiful gorge is another landform recorded by the great explorer, John McDouall Stuart, on his northern journey. Having named Chambers Pillar after an influential patron he named the river which created the gorge, Katherine, after Chambers' daughter.

Katherine Gorge equals in majesty the various canyons of the Hamersleys and the Kimberleys, the steep-sided valleys of the Blue Mountains, and the little-known Lawn Hill Gorge of western Queensland.

Most visitors travel north during the dry winter when conditions are ideal for sightseeing. At that time the river becomes a series of deep pools but boats can still travel along it. At some places one set of boats is abandoned for others anchored in the next pool, ready for the transfer.

In the summer wet when monsoonal rains drench the whole of northern Australia, the river becomes a raging torrent. Waves up to 2 metres in height add to the hazards of the rocks which rise from the river bed and the zigzag course of the stream itself.

Every few hundred metres the high walls abruptly change direction, so the river makes a right-angle turn. These changes in course are due to the massive jointing of the rock. The joints, strongly developed and also widely spaced, provide lines of weakness that are first weathered and then become paths for small rivulets flowing downhill.

With the passage of time these became the beds of the Katherine River and its tributaries, the source of the water being the plateau country of the Northern Territory.

The depth of the gorge walls is due to an older river system being rejuvenated by a rising of the land that made a gently flowing river more vigorous, so cutting a deeper incision into the bedrock.

The splendour of the gorge system was the main reason for the creation of the national park, but the associated plant and animal life is becoming equally important. In the winter mature freshwater crocodiles bask on rocks or sandbanks. In the past they slipped quietly into the water on the approach of a boat but protection for many years has helped them lose their fear of man.

Waterbirds flourish and screw palms and paperbarks line the banks below the red walls. There is a wealth of flowers and trees in the plateau country, including bloodwoods and fan palms, and the display structures of the great bowerbird are often seen, even near the main camping ground of the park.

The rangers have catered for the adventurous by developing a series of walks (ranging from 4 to 36 kilometres in distance) for those who wish to explore the park's 180,000 hectares.

In the dry season this stretch of permanent pools, its waters teeming with fish, was an ideal hunting and gathering area for the Aboriginals and evidence of their activities can still be seen in the many galleries of rock art. Some have faded with the passing of the first people, but some remain, including drawings of crocodiles and striking larger-than-life-

Above and over (pp. 114–15):
Katherine Gorge has been cut through the sandstone rocks by the river that rises in the plateau country of Arnhem Land, then runs west until it reaches the Daly River. It then pours into the sea, west of Darwin. The steep-walled gorge is a major feature of the national park which preserves the most scenic sections.

sized human figures.

It is hoped that future plans to draw more heavily on the waters of the Katherine River will not spoil in any way the present grandeur of this region.

DEVILS MARBLES

The Devils Marbles are fit for giants. Rounded red rocks, they scatter an area 100 kilometres south of Tennant Creek and are divided by the north-south road.

The local Aboriginals described them as eggs laid by the rainbow serpent in his travels across the country.

The original rock suffered the usual fate of all such massive structures by being broken by joints. In the granites of this area the cracks are at right angles to each other and range between 3 and 7 metres apart, so creating a number of large blocks.

Rain, sun and wind erode the entire surface but the edges, where weathering is able to work on two faces, crumble faster. On the corners, where three surfaces meet, the erosion is even more rapid and the once-cubic or rectangular blocks wear into almost perfect spheres or egg shapes. Sometimes a larger egg may split in two along a new joint line.

Wind and rain sweep away the fragments from the base so that the boulders lie on a flat surface like giant marbles.

Their colour is the typical desert red. After leaching of the rock, minerals, particularly iron, are left as a deposit on the surface when the water carrying them

Above:
The Devils Marbles are giant granite boulders which have been rounded by weathering.

Right:
A close-up shows how time has eroded the sandstone of Chambers Pillar.

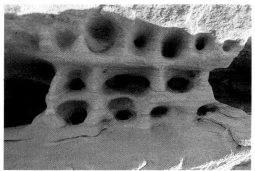

in solution evaporates. In this way is created the almost universal paint that colours both the soil and the rock of arid regions.

These boulders are not unique in Australia. Similar tors are found in a number of places. Every State has its unusual landforms, although none is as dramatic as this collection by the Stuart Highway.

CHAMBERS PILLAR

An imposing pillar of white sandstone, topped with red, stands on the edge of the Simpson Desert. It is one of the outstanding landmarks of the sandridge country surrounding it. Long venerated by the Aboriginals, it was also an important stopping place for early white explorers.

The local Aboriginals explained its origin in the Dreamtime through the coming of a gecko lizard travelling northeast from the Finke River. As was common with such heroes of the long ago he became a towering human who created the landforms of the country as he moved through it.

After many adventures he came on a woman he desired. She was the wrong 'skin' for him, and so by taking her as his wife he broke one of the strictest of moral codes and was outlawed from the tribe.

He went back into the desert country and there turned into rock, still standing high in defiance. His wife, crouching in her shame, became a low hill some 500 metres to the northeast.

So Itirkawara the Dreamtime hero and

Above and over (p. 118):
Chambers Pillar, on the western edge of the Simpson Desert, is a mass of white sandstone with a red ironstone capping. The stone is very soft and easily eroded by wind and rain.

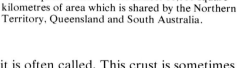

Above, left and over (p. 121):
The Simpson Desert covers almost 80,000 square kilometres of area which is shared by the Northern Territory, Queensland and South Australia.

it is often called. This crust is sometimes on top of soil, sometimes below the surface. It may be made of iron minerals, lime or silica.

Hardpans are called various names. Those rich in iron minerals, sometimes with aluminium ores such as bauxite, are called laterite or duricrust; those with silica are known as silcrete or grey billy. Often the layers below are pallid as the minerals have been leached from them to form the hardpan. Because the tough upper layer resists erosion such residuals become mesas, or tent hills, which gradually wear to a pyramid shape known as a butte, a scree slope of the harder material forming a layer surrounding this remnant.

THE SIMPSON DESERT

Travelling day after day through a seemingly interminable desert of sand dunes, each rising up to 35 metres above the plains between them, and by journey's end to have surmounted more than 1,100 metres might not seem an ideal holiday, yet surprisingly, it can be, and I have enjoyed such an expedition.

The desert and the sea have much in common and have attracted the adventurous all over the world. In both cases there is the feeling of limitless wastes, of cleanliness, and of a horizon which stretches like the rim of a vast blue bowl.

his wife live on in the landscape, part of that unity with the earth which is an innate need for every tribal person if they are to maintain their vitality, and indeed even their existence.

The first European explorer to describe this landform was John McDouall Stuart. He came there on 19 April 1860 and named the landform after one of his Adelaide patrons.

More explorers came in the tracks of Stuart. Ernest Giles wrote '. . . I found it to be a columnar structure, standing upon a pedestal which is perhaps sixty feet high, and composed of loose white sandstone, having vast numbers of blocks lying about in all directions. From the centre of the pedestal rises the pillar, composed also of the same material rock; at its top and for twenty to thirty feet from its summit the colour of the stone is red; . . . The same stone is so friable that names can be cut in it to almost any depth with a pocket-knife'.

The characteristics of the pillar as described by Giles are typical of many parts of Australia where old plains are covered with a tough crust, or hardpan as

The Simpson Desert, which covers almost 80,000 square kilometres of area, is shared by the Northern Territory, Queensland and South Australia, although the Northern Territory has the lion's share. This mass of sand is shaped like a giant equilateral triangle whose base lies against the MacDonnells and whose apex points at Lake Eyre, the drainage basin towards which so many of the inland rivers flow.

Coming from the north, the south, the east and the west, in good years these rivers reach nearer and nearer to Lake Eyre. They usually dump their load of sand along their watercourses; this material dries out and is then moved north by the prevailing winds.

The Simpson Desert is only a sheet of sand, sometimes 35 metres thick and in other places even less, that overlies huge alluvial and lake sediments. It is a young desert, possibly developed in a more arid period that lasted from about 18,000 to a few thousand years ago.

It is only one of the many deserts that fill the central two-thirds of this continent. Most are made of sand ridges: long fingers often running without a break for hundreds of kilometres.

The ridges can be less than 100 metres, or up to a kilometre apart with the interdune areas lined by beds of clay. Water collects here in good seasons and after heavy rains this desert, particularly in its southern and easterly sections, often has more surface water than sand!

There is a rough pattern to the direction these Australia-wide ridges run. Those of the eastern and western deserts have a north-south orientation; those in the north and south lie east-west. So they all follow the directions of the vast anti-cyclonic winds that dominate the weather patterns of central Australia.

The dunes of the Simpson in particular normally show a steeper slope on the eastern side, due to the fact that the strongest winds blow from the southwest. When the winds swing to the southeast, they help keep the tongues of sand moving in a northerly direction.

Most of the dunes seem well fixed by plantlife, only the crests showing living sand, but measurements taken near Bedourie in Queensland show they are moving up to 10 metres a year. This slow drift of sand, rather than encroaching on the coastal cities as was once feared, is fortunately moving away from them.

The sand ranges from white and yellow to a pink and then finally to a deeper red. Towards evening the dunes glow bright red in the slanting light of the sun. It is then and in the early morning that the desert is at its most mysterious and beautiful.

The changing colour is due to the small amounts of clay mixed in the original white river sand. These weather, releasing the iron oxides that provide the typical desert reds.

This small amount of clay often creates cores in the centre of dunes and adds to the interdune areas where slightly richer soil encourages small shrubs and trees to grow, particularly near the eastern edge of the Simpson Desert.

A desert dune typically has cane grass growing on the tops, and, after a good season, mulla-mullas, poached egg daisies and billy buttons. The mid-slopes carry spinifex of various species while hakeas and grevilleas as well as mulga and gidgee often grow at the base and in the areas between the ridges. The occasional salt pans are fringed with saltbush and samphires.

The early history of the Simpson Desert shows it was much lusher than it is today and was the haunt of Aboriginal clans. Even with the coming of the arid cycles, good seasons still allow the Aboriginals to harvest the deserts for animals and plants.

The pastoralists had probed its edges and even travelled the north-south ridges, but the geologist C. T. Madigan organised a massive scientific expedition in the 1930s so making much of this region known to science. He named it after the-then President of the South Australian branch of the Royal Geographical Society of Australasia.

Dr Madigan loved the Red Centre, the Simpson Desert and Lake Eyre in particular, and it was his indomitable and adventurous spirit that led to our present understanding of these remarkable places.

Western Australia

KARRI KINGDOM

To sit yarning around a campfire in the depths of a karri forest is an exhilarating experience. The flames reveal the boles of giant trees and through an occasional gap in the canopy you can glimpse the far-off bright stars. In the morning, as one looks upward to a green roof of leaves, there is a feeling of being overwhelmed by natural beauty comparable to the emotion many experience on seeing the Taj Mahal of India.

In Australia we have few crown jewels of man-made beauty but we do have an abundance of natural jewels, many of them described in this book.

Most of our eucalypts are evergreen and we do not see the dramatic leaf loss of the deciduous trees of the Northern Hemisphere, but we do have the fascinating shedding of bark with the seasons. The splendour of the karri forest in particular cannot be experienced in one viewing as during the course of a year the karri's bark changes from white to glowing orange-yellow.

In its way the karri forest of southwestern Australia is similar to a temperate rainforest with a closed canopy some 60 metres above the ground, although individual trees may reach 86 metres. Below there is a dense mass of small trees and shrubs ranging from light-green karri wattle, yellow and red karri waterbush, karri hazel, plus occasional intruding trees such as jarrah, marri and tingle. All these plants deeply shade the forest floor where only mosses, ferns and other dim-light plants can thrive.

Karri grows only in the wetter places where, although there are the same wet winters and warm summers of the rest of the southwest, more frequent summer showers soften the burning heat. The slopes of valleys are its main home and it grows on a variety of soils ranging from yellowish-brown sandy loams to brown and red clays.

It is a forest of the extreme southwest ranging from Nannup in the north to Bow Bridge in the south, although pockets occur between Margaret River and Augusta and as far to the east as the Porongorup Ranges.

Arguments about the tallest karri abound but one record claims a felled tree measured 104·2 metres. Today's living giants reach around 86 metres and two individual trees have become famous. The Gloucester Tree near Pemberton was climbed by an intrepid forester so that a fire lookout could be built near its top, some 60 metres above the ground. Iron spikes driven into the trunk make a ladder to reach this eyrie. Another tree, 61 metres high, was felled and hauled to Perth where it is now on display in Kings Park overlooking the city.

One karri cut some years ago was 10 metres in girth and measured about a metre above ground level. In those days cutting was by axe and making the first scarf, or wedge-shaped cut in the tree, took five hours. From the other side there were four hours more work with a crosscut saw. The final log cut was 81 metres long.

In terms of plant engineering such a forest king is extraordinarily efficient. It pumps water from the ground to the topmost leaf, and an average tree releases into the air about 150,000 litres of water vapour every year.

The beauty of this hardwood timber brought it into commercial use as it is stiff and tough, stronger than English oak and its colour varies from pale pink to deep red. In many ways the timber rivals jarrah in value and is used in an equally wide variety of ways.

It is sad to think that this timber is suffering the indignity of being converted into woodchips for papermaking; although in theory, at least, this fate is reserved for trees which lack the size or quality needed for sawlogs.

Today's forest covers only about 180,000 hectares, less than half that at the beginning of the century and the last ten years has seen a large drop from the 300,000 hectares of 1974. Even the needs of industry should not overlook the urgent necessity of conserving, as national parks, enough of the best karri forest so that future generations will be able to look up in awe at this magnificent manifestation of nature in the forests of the southwest.

THE JARRAH FOREST

If karri is king, then jarrah is the crown prince. Its virtues are best seen in springtime when this usually rather sombre forest becomes a blaze of colour.

Watching for fires is an important task every summer in the forests of southwest Australia. This giant karri had its top lopped to allow a lookout tower to be built high above the forest.

123

There can be few sights more beautiful than a field of blue leschenaultia lying like a piece of sky on the earth, or the golden blaze of the prickly bitter pea wattle, the deep red of coral vine, the strange shapes of donkey orchids, the gold of guinea flowers and the hundreds of other plants which make the jarrah forest a wildflower garden in spring.

There must be few forests in the world that can offer such a diversity of flowers during this season. The colours are more muted in karri forests but blue hoveas, red flame peas, the pink of karri boronia and the white trails of clematis help to make a gorgeous display.

The natural wonder of both jarrah and karri has led to both forests being appreciated by bushwalkers ever since settlement; and to show a good sample of the country, without the walkers destroying the beauty they come to see, a new trail modelled on the famous Appalachian Trail of North America, has been developed. Called the Bibbulman Track, in honour of the resident Aboriginal tribe, it begins in the Darling Scarp at Kalamunda and runs south to the Boorara Tree, a giant karri near Northcliffe, close to the south coast.

Like karri, jarrah is an Aboriginal word. It was originally pronounced djarryl and corrupted by use into the easier-sounding jarrah. It is interesting to note that in Western Australia a number of common trees are today known by their Aboriginal names, a fashion not followed in the eastern States. Perhaps this was because many of the pioneer families remained on friendly terms with the local Aboriginals, playing with them as children, and adding their words to their own vocabulary. Aboriginals were also used as guides in new country, leading settlers to waterholes, and were useful shepherds on new farms.

The settlers soon learned more than the name of this wonder tree. It was found that here was an almost universal wood, suitable for the most delicate of furniture, or the roughest of piling or blocks for roadmaking. Jarrah proved resistant to rot and was equally resistant to the attacks of wood-devouring termites.

The timber is dense and hard and the reddish colour deepens with age. Its deep red earned it an early name of Swan River mahogany because of a resemblance to Honduras mahogany, an important item of export on the other side of the world. As a result, jarrah was destined to be one of the first exports from this new colony.

The act of declaring the city of Perth began with the cutting of a tree which was probably a jarrah and this tradition of forest destruction has been carried on ever since. The slaughter of the forests continued until just after World War One when governments began to realise what a treasure they had in jarrah and karri. Regeneration began, but by this time the forests had shrunk to one-fifth of their original area. Today the jarrah forest covers some 1,600,000 hectares from New Norcia in the north to the south coast, and inland to the 750 millimetre annual rainfall line.

It grows in pure stands over much of this country but has mixtures of marri on better soils, while on the drier, eastern side it has invasions of the wandoo and

THE SOUTH COAST

Masses of granite and gneissic rocks outcrop along the south coast, creating by their solidity a rugged and spectacular coastline. At the eastern edge are the projections such as Cape Arid and Cape Le Grand, with the town of Esperance dominated by gneissic granite bluffs.

Further to the west near Albany are a number of striking rock structures. At West Cape Howe, the southernmost point on this section of the coast, dark basalt cliffs drop some 70 metres to the ocean. For many months the strong and steady winds of the Roaring Forties crash the long, ocean swells against the rocks, adding to the powerful effect of the landforms themselves.

Additions to previous national parks have now created a magnificent South Coast National Park which covers about 180 kilometres of coastline and an area of more than 100,000 hectares. It includes not only the coastal outcrops but also heathland, and in better soils grow forests of karri and other eucalypts. The curious pitcher plant, some of whose leaves are adapted to form a jug or pitcher to trap unwary creatures, grows in the swampy areas near the coast. The jugs, gay with streaks of green, brown and red, rest on the ground holding in their base the liquid bait in which the victims drown, their bodies later providing nourishment for the plant.

Near Albany are a number of scenic reserves with rock forms such as blowholes, and a natural bridge with a nearby sheer drop to the sea. The granitic gneisses of the area weather to a smooth, rounded shape varying from white and grey to yellow and brown.

york gum which finally replace it further to the east.

The tree has a stringy bark that comes away in strips, a medium height of about 40 metres, and a bole some 2 metres in diameter rising cleanly for about 25 metres when it is growing in good conditions. It thrives on soils covered with a hard surface layer called laterite, a yellowish to red gravel formation which contains varying amounts of the oxides of iron and aluminium.

The thin soils which develop here are infertile, and the dense laterite must be penetrated by the roots, of which jarrah possesses a formidable array. These roots are able to push down to the water table and in many areas this groundwater has accumulated salt, mainly through the rain which brings on average between 60 and 260 kilograms to each hectare of forest annually. Cutting down the trees means that these effective plant pumps stop work; so there is a rise in the water table, bringing the salt to the surface and destroying the growing qualities of the soil.

Western Australia's jarrah forest is facing two threats. First, the ravages of a disease known as cinnamon fungus or 'dieback', a soil-borne disaster that can destroy practically all the trees and shrubs of a jarrah forest. It is as effective a tool of destruction as clearing was in the early days of settlement. A solution to this problem has yet to be found.

Another, and potentially more disastrous threat, is the discovery that rich pockets of bauxite, the aluminium ore scattered through the laterite, are commercially viable. The richer the pockets, the better the growth of jarrah.

Under the onslaught of both dieback and mining for bauxite, jarrah faces an uncertain future. It was summed up by a distinguished Western Australian scientist who, when asked what he thought of the chance of jarrah's survival said bluntly, 'Buy jarrah furniture'.

The eastern States experienced the rise in value of red cedar when the primeval forests had been destroyed. Unless action is taken to conserve them the jarrah forests of the southwest may also be remembered only in the form of magnificent furniture.

THE STIRLING RANGES

Rising like a theatrical backdrop from the cleared lands that surround it, the Stirling Ranges is one of the most beautiful national parks in the West. A wealth of wildflowers adds to its charm; over 800 species have been recorded and the number will probably reach a thousand as research continues.

The floral abundance is not easily explained but one suggestion is that about ten million years ago a shallow sea invaded this southwest corner, converting the high land to islands. The theory of evolution holds that when a large population of animals or plants is separated by some barrier, then varieties living on separate islands may gradually change into new forms, free from the old competition.

The Stirling Ranges is one of the larger national parks in Western Australia with about 115,000 hectares, and the rugged landscape and variety of wildlife make it one of the most popular for both casual visitors and hardy bush walkers and rock climbers. Snow occasionally briefly

covers the peaks in winter while in summer, as the light fades just before sunset, a cloud may form around the peaks and pour towards the foothills like a white blanket. Halfway down it seems to hesitate as though the spirit of the mountain is brooding over the problem of how much cover is needed on a warm night. The cloud then descends, draping the magical Stirlings.

The Ranges are made of ancient sediments—quartzites, slates and shales, yet the surrounding rocks are a much younger series. About 160 kilometres to the east another range in the same line as the Stirlings, but not as high, also consists of old sediments, contrary to the usual rule that the youngest rocks are on top of the older.

The generally accepted explanation for this is that about 1,000 million years ago an invading sea inundated some of the ancient granite rocks of the western shield that covers so much of the State. Erosion from the higher country deposited sand and clays in huge layers of sediment in the sea. As the sea retreated all became dry land once more and due to pressure and drying out, the soft sediments became hard rock. Faults in the earth's crust allowed the block which now forms the Stirlings to sink into the earth. Then erosion wore away the surrounding country and also added younger sediments in new seas, but this particular section was protected, deep below the surface.

By this time the sands and mudstones had become the sandstones, quartzites, shales and slates found in the area today. The land was pushed up once more along the old lines of weakness and the Stirling Range as we know it was created. Erosion then carved the rocks into the spectacular landscape we see today with Bluff Knoll at 1,073 metres as the highest peak.

The chain of other peaks stretches for 65 kilometres east and west but only 15 kilometres from north to south. The one major break in this line of ranges is Chester Pass. The road through it allows visitors to reach the heart of the Ranges, and in passage enjoy the beauty of the area, but full appreciation can be obtained only on foot, when new wildflowers appear every few metres and the majestic mountain scenery unfolds as the visitor climbs higher.

It has been suggested that as most 'national' parks are State-controlled we have no national parks in the strict sense, except one on Christmas Island, Kakadu, Uluru and the Great Barrier Reef Marine Park, all managed by the Australian government. Australia should develop a new system in which both State and Federal governments co-operate to manage special parks in such a way so that they keep all their beauty and interest no matter how popular they become.

These special parks could be called National Heritage Parks and the Stirling Ranges should certainly be among the first of them.

WAVE ROCK

This extraordinary formation was almost unknown, except to local residents who took picnics to it, until an amateur photographer sent in a colour slide for a world competition, organised in America.

Wave Rock near Hyden rears in the air like a massive breaker of stone. Similar curves in stone are found across southern Australia and are due to weathering away of the base of massive rock outcrops.

Right and over (pp. 130–1):
The Pinnacles Desert is now part of the Nambung National Park. These strange pillars of limestone formed in the sand and are revealed only when wind erodes their covering.

He won first prize and this frozen wave of granite near the small country town of Hyden became world famous.

It is equally interesting from a scientific point of view. In his book, *Geomorphology*, Dr C. R. Twidale describes how these flares or overhanging slopes develop and explains that they are due to a special kind of weathering. In the normal process of weathering, debris gathers at the bottom of slopes, carried there by running water and the pull of gravity. In this mixture of sand and larger pebbles water accumulates and, being in contact with the solid granite, continues to work steadily day after day, week after week and year after year, breaking up the rock there much faster than on the slopes nearby which dry out after rain.

It not only eats away at the rock below the soil but also sideways into the rock so that the weathering profile changes from a gentle slope above ground to a steeper gradient below the soil.

When erosion removes this build up of material it leaves behind the start of a wave or flare. As erosion continues to remove the soil around the base of the rock, the wave increases in height. Under certain favourable conditions it can reach the size of Wave Rock. Smaller waves can be found on the side of Ayers Rock near Maggie's Spring and on many granite outcrops in Western and South Australia.

This work of rain, wind, water and sun on etching away at rock surfaces has been described in the story of the Remarkable Rocks in South Australia.

The Wave Rock at Hyden is part of the old weathered plain with a mass of granite rising as a low hill in the shape geologists call a monadnock. This large mass of rock is made of three sections, Wave Rock being part of the north face of Hyden Rock.

There are many weathered pits on the upper surface and from these streams trickle down the slopes carrying with them carbonates of iron and other minerals dissolved from the weathering of granite. The lime used in building water-catchment walls on the top of the rock also adds to the minerals carried by the water.

As a result a series of bands, ranging from light sandy through yellows and browns to rusty reds has developed on the slopes where the water has evaporated and left behind the solids that were in solution. These vertical lines add much to the visual impact of the giant wave rock with its overhang of 15 metres.

Standing under the wave can be exciting, particularly when wind-driven clouds give the illusion that the rock is moving.

The wave is not the only erosion pattern here. There are gnamma holes on the top and circular hollows in isolated boulders. One is called Eggshell Rock, while a cavern near Wave Rock, in tribute to the size of the opening, is called the Hippo's Yawn.

THE PINNACLES DESERT

The Pinnacles is another spectacular landform unknown to most Western Australians until about thirty years ago. In 1956 a Perth historian, Harry Turner, stumbled across a fascinating landform: golden pinnacles of limestone standing like an array of stonehenges on 400 hectares of bare yellow sand.

It was almost hidden from the rough coastal track, but in an area well known to the stockmen of the last century who drove their cattle south to Perth along the eastern edge of the Pinnacles, and often camped at a watering place they called Flourbag Flat.

Harry Turner found that the Pinnacles Desert not only had a forest of rock towers but was also surrounded by interesting heathland plants and animals, small lakes, and a smaller group of pinnacles. The Desert also has magnificent views east to Dandarragan, north to the Nambung Valley, and south to a silhouette of blue hills, which are part of the Darling Scarp.

Pillars of limestone are common on the sandplains, including those on which Perth was built. Bulldozers levelling land for homes, or digging into the sand for swimming pools, often uncover these smooth vertical pillars, while in a few places wind erodes away the sand to reveal them. At the Pinnacles erosion has been severe and stripped away the soil over a large area to create vistas of surprising beauty.

The sandy soil of the coast contains fragments of lime or calcium carbonate as well as silica. In its fall through the air to earth rainwater dissolves some of the carbon dioxide it contains and becomes acidic. Passing through the humus in the surface layers of the land it takes in more of this gas and then begins its gradual passage towards the water table. Here it either begins a slow journey to a lake or river as underground water, or remains lying in the water table. On its way it dissolves the lime fragments.

During the hot dry summer, the water table falls and much of the dissolved lime comes out of solution and forms a lime layer. As the water evaporates it may help cement the sand grains, changing soft soil into harder coastal limestone or eolianite as it is called.

Sometimes the lime consolidates along particular sections of the soil, often following long dead roots of trees and shrubs that provide a convenient channel.

As the years pass, the deposits become thicker. Sometimes water will even pass down a central hole when the root finally rots away, so that inside and outside more layers of lime are laid down until the original pipe, which was only a few centimetres thick, becomes a metre or more in diameter. Consolidation can go on only above the water table as it is only in this damp layer that the lime-charged water can evaporate.

131

This cementation can be rapid—I have seen layers formed over a period of twenty years when I visited a sand dune area to the south of the Pinnacles.

Even when we understand how these pillars are formed, the wonder remains. This forest of golden pillars rising from a hard bed of reddish soil or pale yellow sand, encircled by plant-covered hills carpeted in spring with wildflowers, where grey kangaroos, honeyeaters and occasional brumbies live, is one of the most exciting of landforms, lying hidden in the southwest corner of Australia.

THE HAMERSLEY RANGES

The drive from Roebourne on the coast, past the striking landform of Pyramid Hill, then up the steady rise of the Mount Herbert Road with its Python Pool and old camel track snaking across the gold of seeding spinifex, to the northern edge of the 400 kilometres of the Hamersley Range will always remain vivid in the memory of any visitor.

A huge section of this land of hills and gorges is preserved in the almost 600,000 hectares of the Hamersley Range National Park, the second largest in the state; but the 'look' of the landscape surrounding this magnificent drive should also be preserved so that future generations of

Left:
As the tableland is eroded the first formations are mesas, or 'tent' hills as they are often called in Australia. As erosion continues the flat-topped hills gradually shrink to Pyramid formations called buttes. Pyramid Hill on the main north road in the Pilbara district near Roebourne is a good example of this.

Far left:
The tableland in the Hamersley Ranges has been eroded to create steepsided and spectacular gorges, such as the Weano and Red Gorges.

Below left:
Dales Gorge in the Hamersley Ranges is a great gash in the tableland. Spinifex and other desert plants grow in arid country above it and luxuriant plant growth offers a contrast in the sheltered valley. The freshwater pools are fed by natural sub-artesian flows.

Below right:
Python Pool near the main north road in the Pilbara. Water pythons lurk in deep crevices during the winter and search for ducks and other animals visiting the pools in the warm weather. Python Pool is a reserve.

Australians will be able to see it.

The 'landscape park'—a new idea in Australia but common in many other countries—is a legal way of preserving the 'look' of the countryside without interfering with its normal use by the local people.

The enormous Hamersley iron province as it is called begins on the coast north of Onslow and sweeps inland for more than 500 kilometres. The vast quantities of iron-rich rocks, containing more than 55 per cent of iron, are estimated to contain between 5,000 and 6,000 million tonnes of ore.

The rocks of the area are ancient, most of them about 2,000 million years old. The whole of the Pilbara Region is part of a jigsaw of blocks and basins. Blocks are relatively stable areas that have suffered little change while basins rise and fall over aeons of time.

The Hamersley Basin is a mixture of volcanics including tuffs as well as shales, banded iron formations, sandstones, conglomerates and dolomites and many more. All these rocks were laid down in an ancient sea that filled this 100,000 square kilometre basin. In general the beds slope to the south on the northern edge of the basin but are more folded in the southern sections. Later these beds were invaded by molten granites of about 1,750 million years.

Down the ages erosion, uplift and more erosion produced a terraced plateau in the tableland country with the more folded rocks wearing away to rounded hills. Deep valleys were cut into the land when uplift allowed the rivers of the day to begin grinding into their beds once more, finally producing the gorges we see today with scree slopes rising to almost vertical ramparts.

Probably the most striking of all these are those four gashes in the earth—Joffre, Red, Weano and Hancock—that join in an awe-inspiring meeting. Even these are surpassed in beauty by other gorges. Wittenoom is famous for its long and winding structure whose colour changes with every hour of the day. Near its head is the blue asbestos mine. The mining of that deadly mineral resulted in much misery for the miners and the inhabitants of the town and today the area is almost deserted. A new settlement is to be created well away from the dangerous fibres. The old workings, however, are part of the history of the area and could become part of a landscape park.

Further to the east is Dales Gorge, the best known of all the gorges. The road snakes over the top of the plateau and comes to an abrupt stop before the vertical drop where several hundred metres below glitter bright-green pools fringed with ferns and other water-loving plants. The almost scarlet walls of the canyon, coloured by the formations which have made the Hamersley one of the greatest sources of iron the world has known, are a brilliant backdrop for the pools.

The splendour of these mountains, rivers, and gorges comes to a breathtaking climax during winter and spring. It is then that drifts of wildflowers and blossoming shrubs and trees make the whole area a land of wonder. Mulla mullas push bundles of mauve flowering spikes to the sky and masses of Sturt desert pea cover the ground with scarlet. In creek beds the pea-shaped flowers of the white dragon trees bloom in profusion and desert bluebells, white everlastings and mauve parakeelya add to the riot of colour.

The Pilbara, and the Hamersley Range in particular, will be a source of mineral wealth for hundreds of years, but the beauty of this arid landscape could last forever, as long as we plan wisely and make sure that our industrial needs do not destroy its character.

WOLF CREEK METEORITE CRATER

The kangaroos and wedgetail eagles in northwest Australia a few million, or perhaps only a few thousand years ago, must have had a frightening shock when an object weighing many thousands of tonnes, glowing white hot as it plunged through the air in a great arc, hit the earth and exploded.

When the dust of the explosion finally settled, the kangaroos may have had some difficulty in climbing the steep-sided hill that had appeared as if by magic. The eagles would have had a more dramatic view, as they flew over the almost circular hole made by this cosmic bomb, a depression some 60 metres below the level of the rim and 20 metres below the original land surface, with a diameter of 850 metres!

As the years passed the rain and wind gradually filled the crater with a thin layer of soil, but in that arid climate the sharp rim has remained relatively unchanged. In a central section a circular floor of gypsum and silt holds a small pool after rain and medium-sized trees grow inside the crater.

Searching by scientists has revealed weathered fragments of meteoric iron and resulted in the presently accepted theory that, as pieces of this ironstone material have been found mixed with the broken rocks making the rim of the crater, this huge piece of extra-terrestrial material plunged to earth after the laterite layer so common over much of Western Australia had been formed. There is, however, no exact timing of its arrival.

A search for other fragments resulted in the finding of pieces of nickel-iron meteorites as well as a number of other pieces, one weighing about 100 kilograms. These have been weathered from their original metallic structure into oxides of iron. All have been found in an elliptical area lying to the southwest of the crater and some as far away as about 4,000 metres.

Other fragments have been found

within 100 metres of the west side and one large piece was found 500 metres away in Wolf Creek—the channel that gave its name to the crater.

Because of its huge size this crater has aroused much scientific interest around the world and is regarded as being the closest in appearance to those which can be seen on the surface of the moon.

Meteorites generally become visible as shooting stars when about 100 kilometres above the earth's surface. It is then that friction with the air makes them glow and usually disintegrate into dust. Most disappear, except the larger fragments that are able to survive the heating effect of entry.

Experts think these really big visitors from space arrive at the rate of about forty every million years. As 70 per cent of the earth is water, only about a third strike land where their impact can be discovered. Some scientists claim Wolf Creek as the second largest crater in the world, the largest being the Meteor Crater in the United States. Some other texts, however, place it more cautiously as being one of the biggest craters in the world.

For this reason, and for its lunar-like quality, the crater and its surrounding country was declared a reserve and is listed on the register of the Heritage of Australia. Through increased publicity it is becoming a mecca for tourists as well as scientists.

SHARKS BAY STROMATOLITES

Near the edge of southern Sharks Bay black shapes rise from the water like huge rock bubbles. The area has a primeval look, as though life on earth may have begun here; and in fact, the dark rounded masses, living structures built by a blue-green algae, were among the first life forms of 3,500,000,000 years ago. With grim tenacity they have survived until today.

They are stromatolites, and here in the southeast corner of the bay are the most abundant and diverse examples known from the world's seas. First identified in 1954, they are protected as a special reserve and there are plans to put them forward for World Heritage listing

The Wolf Creek Meteorite has a depression some 60 metres below the level of the rim and 20 metres below the original land surface, and a massive diameter of 850 metres.

because of their scientific importance.

Blue-green algae are a very simple form of life and they flourish here because the waters of Sharks Bay are higher in salt than ordinary sea water. A sand bar keeps out inflow from the sea and the high evaporation rate removes freshwater fast enough to cause the rise in salinity. Algae-eating molluscs and other creatures do not penetrate such hypersaline waters and the blue-green algae are free to grow with few predators.

The living tissues of algal mats flourish on the upper surface and trap sand particles and fragments of shells. A few centimetres below the soft living material the lime dissolves and redeposits in a hard layer so that over thousands of years a pillar of material, perhaps a metre deep, is created.

It seems stromatolites flourish best on a firm foundation and the bottom of the bay in this region has the rocky material they need. Growth is slow; some observations place the increase in height at only half a millimetre a year. This would make the bigger stromatolites hundreds of years old.

These blue-green algae which developed in the early life of the earth became widespread by the end of the Precambrian period, some 600 million years ago, and they were then among the most common fossils. They then declined in importance and today are found in only a few scattered places in the seas of the world.

This most tenacious of life forms has its finest stronghold in Sharks Bay, so it is to be hoped the stromatolites will remain undamaged so that they can be studied and admired by future generations.

MOUNT AUGUSTUS

Which is Australia's largest rock? Most think Ayers Rock; others claim Mount Augustus, east of Carnarvon in Western Australia.

Mount Augustus is about 8 kilometres long, about 4 kilometres wide and 1,106 metres high; Ayers Rock is 3 kilometres by 1·5 kilometres and 1,165 metres high. The former apparently wins the competition, except in height, yet the word 'rock' is meaningless in considering landforms. Hawkesbury sandstone is a rock that covers thousands of square kilometres and the limestone of the Nullarbor Plain is even more extensive.

Neither Mount Augustus nor Ayers Rock are boulders separate from the rest of the country. Both are the flat tops of a much larger area of rock, which in the case of Ayers Rock is hidden below the land surrounding it. Mount Augustus is more obviously linked with the rocks of the surrounding hills.

Geologists describe a landform such as Mount Augustus as a monadnock, after a mountain in New Hampshire in the United States. When a landmass is lifted above the sea, erosion begins and rivers develop along lines of weakness. Short rapid rivers running in narrow gorges gradually widen with age as the river cuts both down and sideways. Finally, as flood plains develop, one river valley meets another and in between them may be left a residual of the erosion which is called the monadnock or isolated hill. Eventually the whole surface becomes a peneplain—which can be translated as 'almost plain'. No surface is ever smoothed entirely flat by erosion, but will always show a pattern of wide river valleys and low hills as evidence of the original eroding forces.

Mount Augustus does not lie isolated on a peneplain as Ayers Rock does, but is surrounded by lower hills. From one aspect it does rise gradually into an impressive landform. Ayers Rock, Mount Connor and the Olgas owe the grandeur of their visual impact to the fact that they rise abruptly from a sea of sand and are impressive from all points of the compass.

Also, unlike the three central Australian landforms, Mount Augustus is not uniform in composition. A layer of coarse sandstone and conglomerates lies on top of schists and granitic rocks. These younger sedimentary rocks show some folding and are the same age as the groups found throughout the Pilbara.

THE KIMBERLEY COAST

'When we had been about a Week, we hal'd our Ship into a small sandy Cove, at a Spring-tide, as far as she would float; and at Low Water she was left dry and the Sand dry without us near half a Mile; for the Sea riseth and falleth here about five fathom.'

So wrote William Dampier in 1688 in his first book *A New Voyage Around the World.*

Dampier made little comment on the beauty of this coastline, but today it is

Left:
Stromatolites are living examples of what is believed to have been the first live organisms to appear on earth, some 3,500 million years ago. The best development of stromatolites in the world is believed to be here at Sharks Bay and the area is proposed for nomination as a World Heritage site.

Right:
Surveyor's Pool at the Mitchell River Plateau.

Top:
Windjana Gorge, whose cave walls were used for painting sacred Aboriginal art.

Above:
Prince Regent River at the Prince Regent Reserve, which has recently been declared a sanctuary for wildlife and covers more than 600,000 hectares.

Right:
The Mitchell River Plateau is now being surveyed for its bauxite deposits and plans are being made for a deepwater port.

Over (pp. 140–1):
The Mitchell River Falls at the Mitchell River Plateau.

regarded as one of the most colourful and spectacular in Australia.

This section of the Kimberley Coast is a deeply dissected plateau of ancient rocks dominated by sandstones; its flooding by the sea created a seascape of deep blue water surrounding a maze of islands and red rocks that rise steeply from the shoreline.

Being both infertile and difficult of access it was undeveloped until mining interest in the area resulted in more exploration. The Mitchell Plateau is now being surveyed for its bauxite deposits and plans are being made for a deepwater port. Both this and the Prince Regent Plateau are flat-bedded, deeply jointed sandstone and this contributes to the rugged nature of the country. Helicopters have solved the difficulties of land travel and parties now land in areas once almost impossible to study.

The Prince Regent Reserve is a

recently declared sanctuary for wildlife which covers more than 600,000 hectares. It was dedicated after a scientific committee reported, 'without doubt, the Prince Regent River could become one of the world's outstanding scenic and natural history reserves'.

The plateau in this area slopes to the west and is between 400 and 550 metres above sea level. A striking gorge cut by the Prince Regent River runs into the land-locked Saint George Basin.

Further south is the iron ore mining centre of Yampi Sound, also called Iron Sound as it holds two islands rich in iron ore, Koolan and Cockatoo. The iron ore of Yampi is the mineral known as hematite and occurs as rich lenses. It first became known to white settlers when the pearling fleets used lumps of ironstone for ballast in their luggers.

The flooding of the coast by the sea means deep water is close inshore and ore

ships can be loaded without expensive wharves. Work to develop the mine began in 1939 but was halted by the war. Full development came in 1944 when 10,000 tonnes were shipped to Newcastle and exports continued to the present but the mines are now coming to the end of their commercial life.

Yampi Sound has a rim of the islands mentioned, as well as Irvine and Bathurst, and these are all members of the Buccaneer Archipelago, a group of more than 800 islands, which earned their name because of William Dampier's visit on his buccaneering venture.

The huge tidal movements, which are one of the world's highest ranges (up to 11 metres tall) attracted pirates. Here they ran their ships ashore on high spring tides and cleaned them at neap. Once the hull was cleared of marine growths and a new spring tide allowed it to be refloated, the ship was ready for more raiding.

Above:
An aerial shot of the Lake Argyle area in the Kimberleys.

Left:
Tidal races in the Buccaneer Archipelago.

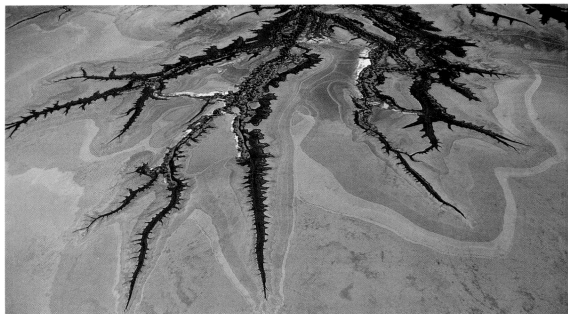

Top:
The Cockburn Ranges in the Kimberleys.

Above:
Hidden Valley in the Kimberleys.

Above right:
Coastal floodplains in the Kimberleys.

Above far right:
King George Sound on the Kimberley coast.

Right:
The Bungle Bungle has become well known only in the last few years. It is a remarkable place of eroded hills whose horizontal sandstones and conglomerates are darkened by lichens and mosses.

The movement of the tides causes racing seascapes as torrents of water pour through narrow gaps between the islands of the Sound. Most of the islands are well forested and offshore coral reefs provide good fishing. It must be one of the most scenic backgrounds of any iron ore mine in the world.

BUNGLE BUNGLE

A remarkable name for a remarkable landscape—an area of mountains and plains with winding rivers that flow only in the wet. In summer, during monsoonal showers, every rushing stream forms a series of cascades. It is a pattern which, over aeons of time, has eroded away the mountain rocks to create the present plains and gorges.

The rocks are made of material eroded from the mountains to the north. This took place in the Devonian Period, some 350 million years ago, and the mixture of sand, pebbles and boulders laid down in the lakes of the period finally became the present-day sandstones and conglomerates.

Although hardened by pressure and time, these still lie horizontally in much the same fashion as when they were deposited hundreds of millions of years ago, and this regularity has helped create the beauty of the present landscape.

From a distance long bands of black and white, running horizontally kilometre after kilometre, make the Bungle Bungle look man-made, with the chasms as walls and the domes like the roofs of an ancient city. The bands of colour result from the different permeabilities of the layers of conglomerate and sandstone.

As the monsoon rain falls it penetrates the earth through cracks in the rock. Slowly it travels down until it reaches the water-table deep in the earth, to join the rivers on the long journey to the sea. Where the rock allows the water an easy passage it seeps along, soaking all the sand grains until it finally reaches the open. Here during the summer wet, the combination of sand, water and sunlight allows algae and lichen and sometimes mosses and other plants do flourish. With the winter dry the plants die, a band of black showing where their remains cling to the rock.

Where the rocks are impermeable they remain a dull white. So nature creates the banded appearance, a spectacular feature of the landscape.

Added to the mountain's strange appearance is the grandeur of 400-metre high cliffs with narrow gorges, winding inland. There is often at the apex a waterfall cascading to the valley floor. Surrounding this huge area of dissected mountain ranges are desert plains where occasional outliers of rocks push up like islands in a sea of spinifex and sand.

The origin of the name, Bungle Bungle, remains a mystery, although the sound is

Aboriginal. The ranges are fairly barren in wildlife terms and so far no traces of human artwork or campsites have been found, apart from the remains of the cattle stations taken up in 1902 by stockmen who were too late to lay claim to the good country nearby.

The land-hungry latecomers accepted a 56,000 hectare lease on what was left, yet the soil was so poor that the settlers were finally defeated. In 1967 the government took over the lease, dedicating it as an area for native plants to protect the catchment of Lake Argyle against overstocking and subsequent soil erosion.

An Aboriginal called Major began a brief war against the white settlers in 1908 and at times he used the Bungle Bungle as a hideout. In a final battle Major and his companions were killed.

So this bizarre landscape, so recently rediscovered, seems likely to become a tourist mecca of the near future.

Certainly everyone in our party who visited the Bungle Bungle earlier this year agreed that it is the most extraordinary landscape in Australia.

WINDJANA GORGE, TUNNEL CREEK AND GEIKIE GORGE

A dolphin swimming towards the Great Barrier Reef off the Queensland coast would see it as a huge wall, barring the way from the open ocean. A person swimming over it sees it as a maze, and there is little evidence of the depth of coral and other marine life that makes the great wall.

In northwest Australia a tourist can see at once the enormity of such a barrier reef—one that developed 350 million years ago and today rears up as the massive wall of rock which makes up the Geikie and Oscar Ranges. For this wall is a barrier reef converted into hard limestone rock which still contains the fossils of the plants and animals that created it. The barrier stretches for about 300 kilometres from east to west, along the northern edge of the Canning Basin. It was part of a U-shaped reef complex which ran westward into the present ocean, then north and finally east again to its end near Wyndham where an outcrop still remains.

This great barrier reef of the ancient Devonian sea was made of different life forms than those which created the Great Barrier Reef of today. While a modern reef is made up mainly of algae, which secretes lime as a binding agent, and corals, Devonian reef corals were overshadowed by algae and colonial animals that resembled corals, but are now all extinct.

This platform of marine life grew in an ocean which varied from shallow to 200 metres deep and the reefs ranged in size from a few hectares to hundreds of square kilometres. Their total depth, shown by the walls of rock today, was due

to the fact that the land was steadily sinking, but at a rate which allowed the reef building organisms to keep pace and remain near the surface.

An international group of geologists hailed this fossil great barrier reef of the Canning Basin as 'one of the most spectacular examples known in the world of an exhumed Paleozoic barrier reef belt'.

Various river systems now cut through the ranges creating gorges of which the best known are Windjana, Brooking and Geikie. As yet only these breaks in the ranges have been reserved as national parks, which is unfortunate as the whole area has a wealth of geological and wildlife interest, while paintings in the caves and overhangs, particularly on the northern face, make this one of the great Aboriginal art areas of Australia.

Windjana Gorge

This break in the hills that runs 4 kilometres through 90 metre high limestone cliffs 'must rank among the world's classic geological localities' said geologist Dr Phillip Playford. In its towering walls the scientific relationships between the various elements which built the ancient barrier reef can be studied in a detail unavailable elsewhere.

In terms of Aboriginal history Windjana is a most important site as from earliest times the cave walls were used for painting sacred art. The wandjinas (the spelling of Aboriginal names tends to vary with the authority writing the text as the people had no written language and the first white settlers wrote such names phonetically) are the most famous of the spirits of the Kimberley region.

They are usually depicted as human figures, often as tall as 6 metres, wearing an elaborate head-dress. Wandjinas are the spirits that control the clouds which bring the life-restoring monsoonal rains of the summer wet, so they were obviously important elements in the original religion.

In his classic book on these paintings anthropologist Dr I. M. Crawford points out that a whole range of figures can be found in the Kimberley, from those complete with body, through a second stage where only the head and shoulders remain, to those where only the halo surrounding the face is kept. The final illustrations, being only a mass of concentric lines with an eye in the centre, are purely symbolic.

Some fanciful Europeans have seen these spirits of the clouds as spacemen in helmets, coming to earth to educate the Aboriginals in a better way of living—an interpretation which could be seen as insulting to people who coped admirably with Australia's resources and difficult environment until the arrival of Europeans, and their sophisticated ways.

But the Aboriginals did not give up their way of life without a struggle. An Aboriginal hero of the last century, Sandamara, fought a guerilla war in these

Left:
Windjana Gorge is cut through the range by the Lennard River, which can be a haunt for freshwater crocodiles.

Above and above right:
Tunnel Creek is a natural tunnel through the Geikie and Oscar Ranges. It runs for 750 metres through the limestone range and was a hiding place for the Aboriginal freedom fighter, Sandamara.

Right, far right and over (pp. 150–1):
Geikie Gorge, about 20 kilometres northeast of Fitzroy Crossing in the Kimberleys, is a canyon cut by the floodwaters of the Fitzroy River. The gleaming white walls of the 8 kilometre long gorge are broken in places by tumbles of earth and limestone boulders.

ranges for over three years in a vain endeavour to drive all the intruding whites out of the northwest. An all-day battle was fought in Windjana Gorge itself, with Sandamara and his army sheltering from the fire of police and settlers in caves in the limestone.

This gorge is cut through the range by the Lennard River and during the dry season the deeper sections remaining as pools are the haunt of freshwater crocodiles. When the eucalypts and paperbarks are flowering hundreds of thousands of black fruit bats roost in the trees in the gorge and fly out at dusk in a spectacular mass of leathery wings that stretch about a metre from tip to tip.

Well-preserved fossils, relics of the marine life of this ancient coral sea, can be seen in the walls of the gorge.

Tunnel Creek

The Aboriginal fighter, Sandamara, used as a hiding place another remarkable landform 30 kilometres southeast of Windjana Gorge. It is a natural tunnel 3 to 12 metres high and about 15 metres wide which runs for 750 metres through the backbone of the limestone range.

A break in the roof about halfway through allows a visitor to climb to the crest of the range. The creek that cut its way through, and springs, keep some water flowing even in the dry winter.

Stalactites developing from the roof add to the spectacle of the cave, particularly near the north entrance where the tunnel is much larger than further in.

The southern entrance once held an Aboriginal graveyard with fragments of skeletons, including skulls. There were also sharpening stones for spearheads and axes as well as many artefacts which disappeared once the gorges and the tunnel became important tourist centres.

Geikie Gorge

Geikie Gorge, some 20 kilometres northeast of the settlement of Fitzroy Crossing, was cut in the Geikie and Oscar Ranges by the Fitzroy River. Its source in the Hann Range runs for some 1,000 kilometres before discharging into the sea and its total catchment area is slightly larger than Victoria.

Geikie and Katherine Gorges are the two most visited examples of these landforms in Australia. They both have very different qualities so it is impossible to say which is the most striking or scientifically interesting.

The national park that preserves Geikie Gorge is small, covering only the 8 kilometre long gorge and the edges of the range which enfold it.

The gleaming white limestone of the walls is polished each floodtime by the rushing waters of the river. During the dry season the water level sinks, leaving about 16 metres of smooth white walls of limestone above the river. Fossils of the algae and other organisms that created the reef can then be seen.

The water has dissolved out caverns in the rock to produce beautiful vistas; trees and shrubs grow on the ledges, and patches of sand line the gorge. They include cadjeputs, river redgums, freshwater mangroves, Leichhardt trees, screw palms, and native figs and native passionfruit vines that climb over the shrubs.

Although the sea is some 300 kilometres from the pools, the water contains seagoing creatures such as sharks, sawfish

and stringrays. There are also the more usual barramundi and archer fish. It is these attractions that make Geikie Gorge one of the natural wonders of the north.

THE EIGHTY MILE BEACH

'. . . nothing has been discovered but a barren, bare, desolate region; at least along the coast and as far as they have penetrated into the interior . . .' was the discouraging report made by a Dutch administrator at Batavia in 1697 to his superiors in Holland.

Much of the western coastline seen from a ship's deck is sandy, even the hill tops are often buried under a massive white sheet of sand.

The Eighty Mile Beach on the northwest coast is part of the landform-soil region in Western Australia called Carnegie, after the explorer who wrote the classic book, *Spinifex and Sand.* These sandy deserts begin in the south with the Great Victoria Desert. This joins the Gibson Desert that links with the Great Sandy Desert, reaching the coast on the Eighty Mile Beach. (Until 1946 it was called the Ninety Mile Beach but the name was changed because of confusion with a stretch of the same name in Victoria.)

The masses of sand in this vast desert are heaped into ridges that run for

hundreds of kilometres; one stretch of 320 kilometres has been recorded, although usually they are shorter.

In the beach area a long unbroken series of ridges lie parallel to the sea. The whole of the land is almost treeless and has no rivers. The massive tidal movements mean that at low water the sea lies several kilometres from the beach and the early pearlers were able to find pearl shells by the technique called dry shelling, where a searcher walks over the sand at low tide.

Although it is largely a barren and desolate region and almost uninhabited, along the coast the slightly greater rainfall, aided by dewfall, allows sheep stations to survive.

Left:
The Great Sandy Desert is the western section of a huge sand dune and stony pavement area that covers the central third of Australia. Most of the sand is stabilised with plantlife, but in some areas it is on the move. Blown along by the wind it creates ripples in the surface.

Below:
Tracks on the Eighty Mile Beach show in the morning where a female turtle had climbed the night before above the high-tide mark, dug a nesting pit and laid her eggs, then headed back to the sea. The disturbed area is where the eggpit has been covered.

153

South Australia

MURPHY'S HAYSTACKS

We tend to see plant, animal or human shapes in the forms sculpted by nature. In Australia we have Dog Rock, the Three Sisters, Mount Elephant and many others. The granite rock outcrops called Murphy's Haystacks, that cover an area of some 20 hectares, 14 kilometres east of Calca, are another. They sound like a touch of Ireland in the Australian bush, but the name came because in the distance the rock outcrops look like big haystacks and Denis Murphy first developed the farm in the Calca district.

The Heritage of Australia states that Murphy's Haystacks 'include flared slopes, tafoni, platforms, rillens and pitting, which are all significant sculptured forms'.

Tafoni are caves or caverns hollowed in tors of this kind. This sort of weathering—mainly chemical but assisted by other erosional forces—is found in many other parts of Australia, so it is worth explaining how an apparently solid and hard rock such as granite can gradually be worn away by the gentle probing of rain, wind, sun and air.

At the basis of all landscape sculpting is the old saying, 'constant dripping wears away the hardest stone'. Just as the tiny hammer blows of drop after drop of water gradually wear away rocks, so too does expansion from the heat from daylight sun followed by contraction caused by the chill of the night.

As well, even the most solid of rocks

Left and below:
Because of their rounded shape this collection of granite rock outcrops east of Calca became known as Murphy's Haystacks.

has fractures, or joints, as they are called. These may be caused during the cooling of a molten rock into solid form, by the earthquake shocks produced by our restless earth, by the actual slumping of areas as a continent settles into a new equilibrium, or as one plate carrying its burden of a continent moves steadily forward to collide with another plate.

Such massive movements of the earth's crust began when it first formed and will continue in the thousands of millions of years that stretch ahead of us.

Hammer blows are the most obvious in terms of shattering a solid rock, but far more destructive are the chemical changes caused by water penetrating into cracks, taking with it the oxygen of the air and changing the nature of minerals so that they crumble and dissolve. This is discussed in the formation of the sculptural forms of Remarkable Rocks on Kangaroo Island.

Tafoni carved in Murphy's Haystacks contain wind-blown sediments that have been dated as having been formed some 33,000 years ago—showing that the tafoni were created at least before then.

Rillen are gutters produced by a combination of the weathering already described and the erosion from water pouring down the tors towards lower areas.

On the surface of all such granite rock outcrops, chemical erosion digs weather pits. When these deepen gnamma holes are created. (Gnamma is an Aboriginal word for such hollows that often held valuable water, even in the hottest summer.) Gnamma holes tend to enlarge below a slightly harder surface, so an opening no larger than a person's head or even hand may be the entrance to a small cave holding thousands of litres of water. To prevent animals falling in and fouling the water, the Aboriginals closed them with a flat slab of rock or the branch of a tree.

White settlers, equally keen to preserve the water, shut off the larger gnamma holes with metal doors or similar covers. Many an outback traveller had reason to be grateful for a gnamma hole.

Finally, the flared slopes of Murphy's Haystacks are similar to those better-known ones along the edge of Ayers Rock at Maggie's Pool. The most famous of all is Wave Rock at Hyden in Western Australia and the way they are formed is described in the section on Wave Rock.

THE NULLARBOR PLAIN

'One of the geographical wonders of the world' was the verdict of a famous Australian scientist, yet many Australians think of it as a long, dreary stretch to be covered as quickly as possible, either by road or rail.

Those who camp on the Nullarbor Plain can wake in the morning and watch the sun rise over a majestic landscape that has no hill or tree to break the sweep of earth and sky. In a good season you can drive hour after hour over ground carpeted with flowers while pipits and songlarks pour out a continuing melody overhead.

Geologically it is a wonder. The plain is incredibly flat, shown by the fact that one straight stretch of the transcontinental railway runs for 500 kilometres. This uniformity is due to the limestone rocks being almost horizontally bedded. About 500 metres deep they are thought by some scientists to be a sea floor exposed when the water retreated. Others think that as the beds are horizontal perhaps a 100 metres of limestone has been stripped away by erosion since its raising.

Thin soil hardly covers the limy bones of the rock, yet in a good season plantlife covers much of the plain and feeds the sheep that still graze in many areas. Indeed, summer bushfires can be a danger, particularly after a good season.

Recent studies show there is a wealth of wildlife in this sea of saltbush, bluebush, speargrass, and woodland of western myall and other trees, particularly along the southern edges.

The latest research has identified about 100 species of birds, six native mammals, twenty-seven reptiles and even one frog among the back-boned animals of the region. Fortunately several national parks have been reserved in both South Australia and Western Australia and the wildlife flourishes in them, untroubled by competition from grazing stock.

There are no large rivers because limestone allows rain to sink in quickly. Although the rainfall is low (only about 200 millimetres annually) the water is charged with carbon dioxide that can dissolve lime and the shallow hollows called dongas are very common on the northern sections of the plain.

They are generally oval or circular hollows, up to 800 metres in diameter and 3 metres deep. Along the southern sections of the plain they are often up to 200 metres across and sometimes more than 30 metres deep.

There are also caves. Shallow ones are found all over the plain, but like the dongas are more common in the north. The deep caves are striking; two of the most famous are Cocklebiddy Cave and Koonalda Cave.

Cocklebiddy is about 360 metres long, 30 metres wide and descends to a low 90 metres below the ground. At the lower levels it is a lake.

The same is true of Koonalda, one of the most remarkable places in Australia. Aboriginal man, some 20,000 years ago, climbed down the cavern into the darkness, travelling 300 metres in the underground system, crawling at times through narrow passages to mine lumps of flint.

At the very end, past the flint mine, there is a hollow the size of a large room. Here the soft limestone wall, easily marked by a steady stroking of human fingers, has been decorated by these miners of long ago. Their only light would have been primitive torches, yet they marked the walls with an almost complete mural of meandering grooves. It is perhaps the earliest art gallery in the world. To sit on the floor of this room and look at the walls by torchlight is one of the most moving experiences Australia has to offer.

Most parts of the Nullarbor also have those remarkable physical features called blowholes. Estimates of their number vary from between 10,000 and 100,000. At certain times every day, air rushes out of each hole in the underground caverns; at other times it rushes in. An early explorer, Arthur Mason, said 'in some the sound is like rushing water, in others like a train at full speed, and again like the noise of an approaching hurricane . . .'

These air movements have nothing to do with the sea, but are caused by differences in pressure caused by the air in the caves being warmer or colder than that of the atmosphere above. The rush of air blowing out will stand on end the hair of anyone leaning over a hole.

There is no general agreement on the boundaries of the Nullarbor Plain. It is shared by South Australia and Western Australia some 300 kilometres east and 350 kilometres west of the border, and ranges about 250 kilometres north until the limestone disappears under the sand of the Great Victoria Desert.

To the south the plain ends abruptly in a long line of cliffs that make the Great Australian Bight. Edward John Eyre wrote 'there was a grandeur and sublimity in their appearance that was most imposing; stretching out before us in lofty unbroken outline, they present the singular and romantic appearance of massy battlements of masonry, supported by huge buttresses, and glittering in the morning sun which had now risen upon them and made the scene beautiful . . .'.

The traveller on the Eyre Highway can stop in a number of places and admire the long line of scalloped cliffs reaching for the horizon in both directions. The

Right:
This aerial shot shows well what a long and flat plain the Nullarbor is.

156

constant battering of the waves driven by
the Roaring Forties is steadily
undercutting the almost 100-metre high
limestone ramparts.

Few people realise there are equally
dramatic views on the border near Eucla
where drifting sand has collected into
dunes, some as high as 100 metres. This
drifting sand overwhelmed the old
telegraph station at Eucla. Before the
coming of the white settlers the sand was
firmly held by dune plants, but the teams
of camels, herds of goats, and the
ubiquitous rabbit, removed these binding
agents and the sand was set free.

THE COORONG

Coorong, the Aboriginal name of the area
means 'neck' and is an apt description of
this huge stretch of water, which is some
100 kilometres long and only about
2 kilometres wide, and is broken at the
northern end where the mighty Murray
River enters the sea through Lake
Alexandrina.

A dense population of Aboriginals,
possibly an average of one person for
each 2·5 square kilometres, lived well
here on a variety of marine products such
as the goolwa cockle, (called pipi in New
South Wales and ugari in Queensland).
Middens of old shells are a feature of the
dune regions of the Younghusband
Peninsula and these molluscs seem to be
just as common today as they were in the
past. Waterbirds and fish caught in the
waters of the Coorong would also have
provided ample food.

Yet the first white settlers thought of
the area as desolate. Julian Tennison-
Woods, writing in the last century, said
'The beach is the most uniformly low and
wretched looking in Australia . . . a
worthy outwork of a terrible desert which
lies inland, . . . as impenetrable as the
beach is unapproachable . . .'.

Today we think differently. After
camping on its shores, exploring the
islands famous for pelican rookeries, and
flying over it, I can only agree with Colin
Thiele who, in quoting George Eliot that
certain regions should be preserved as
hunting grounds for the imagination, said,
'I know of no place on earth where this is

more applicable than the Coorong'.

The structure of the Coorong, as developed during the last 150,000 years, is most complex. Today's narrow stretch of water, very saline at the northern end, with separate salt lakes at the southern, is divided from the sea by the sand dunes of the Younghusband Peninsula and set in a system of barriers formed by beach dunes.

There are more than twenty of these, fixed in place by plants, and up to 30 metres high, all roughly parallel to the coast and stretching inland for about 100 kilometres. It is easy to see that these are all sites of former 'Coorongs' as changes in the level of the land, as well as that of the sea, created the conditions needed for lakes to form between dunes. The sands would at first have been mobile, but gradually cemented by water charged with carbon dioxide dissolving the lime in the soil and depositing it once more as a binding agent.

The twenty present-day barriers mark the site of higher sea levels over the last few hundred, thousand years. Ice ages wax and wane and so cause sea levels to fall and rise as water is taken out by ice

sheets or given back when the ice melts.

When ice ages 'locked up' vast amounts of fresh water, huge areas of continental shelf were exposed and provided an ideal source for sand accumulations found in the area today.

Some 6,000 years ago the sea reached its present level with the waters of the Coorong trapped by the sand dunes thrown up from the sand exposed by the previous lower sea levels. Not that any stability is ever permanent—the Murray mouth has changed many times. After white settlement changes became even more rapid through the clearing of tree and shrub cover and the introduction of new grazing animals including the most destructive pest of all, the rabbit. A survey by the Nature Conservation Society of South Australia found ninety-two alien kinds of plants, representing 35 per cent of the total 258 species collected. This indicates the settlers not only caused destruction of the plant cover but also changed its original quality.

All these factors have produced unhappy results in many areas. Blowouts of sand are common on the

Younghusband dunes; some may be 200 metres long, 60 metres wide and 10 metres deep. In addition, the barrage built to keep the freshwater of Lake Alexandrina separate from the salt water of the Coorong has changed the quality of the water. Drainage schemes along the eastern side of the Coorong have also had their effect.

In spite of all these changes the Coorong remains a haven for wildlife, particularly birds.

REMARKABLE ROCKS

The Remarkable Rocks of Kangaroo Island certainly deserve their name. They cluster on a bare surface like modern forms displayed in a gallery. Their sculptural quality becomes even more marked at close quarters when details of the fretting and texture of these strange rocks can be examined.

They are the kind of granite found at Victor Harbor on the mainland and, as with granites everywhere in the world, their main minerals are glassy, greyish quartz, felspar, and mica. On weathering, the quartz becomes the familiar grains of sand found on most beaches; white felspar weathers away to clay, and black mica, like the quartz, is resistant to erosion.

How was it that this granite, deep in the underground hundreds of millions of years ago, became these huge sculptured blocks? Over aeons of time the overlying rocks were eroded away until the great granite mass was exposed. Water, the universal solvent, began its work, attacking the minerals of the granite, working faster along the regular cracks of joints that are found in the most massive-looking rock.

By the time the Remarkable Rocks were stripped clean of overlying soil they had the rounded shape seen in the Devils Marbles of the Northern Territory. The joints that fractured the rock tend to lie at right angles to each other, so creating a number of giant cubes. Water in the soil penetrates the surface cracks and works more swiftly on the corner of each piece so there is a gradual rounding of the whole as fragment after fragment lifts and crumbles into soil.

The chemical effect continues, particularly in places out of the sun where rain collects and the rock remains damp. As the hollows deepen, more water

remains and caverns appear. No granite is completely even in texture so the sculpting is not uniformly smooth and strange patterns evolve.

The cave openings tend to be towards the north-northeast, away from the prevailing south-southwest winds that tend to keep that side of the rock dry and relatively unaltered.

The site of these rock forms and the huge granite dome plunging into the sea on its southern side is dramatic. Even the most famous of the world's man-made sculptures cannot achieve this combination of form and place.

ADMIRALTY ARCH

The Remarkable Rocks are part of the famous Flinders Chase National Park, almost 60,000 hectares of the western end of Kangaroo Island. This park was first reserved in 1919 and has become one of South Australia's best-known tourist spots.

Remarkable Rocks are about 14 kilometres south of the ranger's station in the park, and 10 kilometres to the west is the Cape De Couedic Lighthouse, built in 1909. Further along the cliff tops is another striking landform called Admiralty or Admirals Arch.

The power of the sea gradually wore away the rocks to create the arch and it makes a frame for the giant waves pushed by the Roaring Forties on their sweep around the globe. The floor of ancient sediments is slippery and walking through can be treacherous. The archway is decorated high overhead with a chevaux-de-frise of stalactite spikes.

Sturdy hair seals and their more graceful cousins, the fur seals, swim in the stormy seas or perch precariously on wave-swept boulders.

Although most of the rocks of Kangaroo Island are ancient sediments similar to those in the floor of this arch, dune limestone has covered them in more recent times through strong winds blowing a mixture of sand and shells

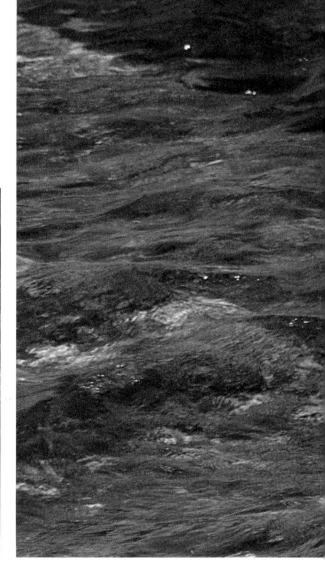

Top left:
Admiralty Arch frames Admirals Cave near the western end of Kangaroo Island.

Above:
Sea lions on Kangaroo Island.

Left:
Remarkable Rocks. Nature has produced these striking sculptures in granite using air, wind and water as cutting tools.

inland. Gradually, through the dissolving power of rainwater saturated with carbon dioxide, this scattered lime was first dissolved and then redeposited to cement the mass into a rock called dune limestone or eolianite.

Yet nature is forever tearing down what it has so patiently built. The lime in the eolianite is once more dissolved by ground water and removed to form caves below the surface or structures such as Admiralty Arch. Yet again nature starts to build as rainwater trickles down, dissolving the lime of the roof and depositing it on the ceiling.

Over hundreds and perhaps thousands of years the lime builds up, particle by particle, into the stalactite spears that hang menacingly from the Arch.

The dark grey of the quartzites of the floor, smooth polished by the sea and glittering like glass in certain lights, the sombre portcullis of the roof and the brilliant blue of the sea seen through the archway make this one of the most splendid of the landforms along the southern coast of Kangaroo Island.

STURTS STONY DESERT

Sturt's name is scattered over central Australia: it has been given to a physical feature, Sturts Stony Desert; South Australia's floral emblem is the Sturt pea; and rock formations near Adelaide are called the Sturt group by geologists.

Sturts Stony Desert as a landscape

epitomises the toughness of this explorer, who is famous in Australian history for his Murrumbidgee-Murray expedition in 1829 and the incredible central Australian journey begun in 1844 during which he found the 'stone-clad desert' that today bears his name.

The central two-thirds of Australia is a single arid area, the central section of it, a desert. Particular sections of this desert have been named, usually for the first explorer, or by them in honour of some past or possible future patron. The limits of these sections are rarely exact; Sturts Stony Desert can be regarded as being an area in northeast South Australia lying between Cooper Creek and the Diamantina.

This plain was first crossed by white

Top, above and left:
The last members of the Burke and Wills expedition wandered along Cooper Creek before their death. Its headwaters are in Queensland and its final destination Lake Eyre; Cooper Creek, like most inland rivers, is usually dry.

Over (pp. 164–5):
Sturts Stony Desert was named in tribute to one of the toughest of our inland explorers. In this most fearsome of all Australian deserts it was not the sand which defeated him but the stone gibbers, the heat and the lack of water.

explorers in 1845 when Charles Sturt described it as an 'iron region'. The appalling heat, the barren country, and the lack of water finally defeated his chances of finding the Holy Grail of desert explorers, the 'inland sea', but he spoke of sandhills thrusting up like ocean cliffs and gibbers which reminded him of shingle on an English beach. Possibly his dream of finding a desert sea led to his dwelling on maritime phrases.

The appearance of the Stony Desert baffled Sturt. In his journal he was driven to confess he 'was at a loss to divine its nature' and its extensive gibber plains, covered with stones ranging from a few millimetres to sizeable boulders, still offer mysteries to the scientists.

Gibber plains are named for the rocks with which they are strewn, gibber being an Aboriginal word for stone. Often the gibbers are covered with a fine polish called desert glaze, the origin of which is in dispute. It is partly due to chemical weathering depositing minerals on the surface and partly from polishing by wind-driven sand.

Dr C. R. Twidale, a geographer, says of the gibber plains and the Stony Desert that about 50 million years ago the Lake Eyre Basin was a region of low relief, typical of much of arid Australia today. It was then that chemical weathering dissolved out silica to redeposit it as a mantle on the surface above a stone-free clay subsoil. Many a desert traveller has found to his cost that if his vehicle breaks through the gibber rock layer it will sink, hopelessly bogged in the clay below.

This silcrete or 'grey billy' layer as it is sometimes called, consists of quartz grains set in a mass of fine-grained quartzose material. Because of its hardness, silcrete resists erosion and forms the capping that protects the upper surface of the tent hills and tablelands so common in the area. When erosion undermines the clay, then the hard layers tumble as scree slopes that spread over the plain, forming gibber.

Some geologists think the silcrete layer is heaved up from layers in the clay in the same way as the famous gilgais (saucer-shaped depressions often up to 100 metres in diameter), which are found in clay country.

Dr Twidale also believes that in this particular basin the soil may have been covered with plants rich in silica. The particles of this mineral would

accumulate in the soil as the years passed.

Today the gibber plains are widespread in arid Australia, with Sturts Stony Desert as the core, and are scattered over much of northeast South Australia, nearby Queensland and New South Wales.

Yet this desert is not all gibber plain. Sturt commented on the 'stupendous and almost insurmountable sandridges of a fiery red', where streams flood after heavy rain, valleys with soil nourish trees, shrubs and grasses. In such hollows the 100 millimetres of annual rainfall is concentrated to produce a much wetter soil where trees such as river redgums and coolabahs can grow. Mulgas, with their unusual relative, the gidgee, whose flowers produce an unpleasant odour when wet, are also features of this desert.

MOUNT GAMBIER

The Aboriginals of western Victoria and southeast South Australia lived through some exciting times 600 to 1,400 years ago and must have witnessed some spectacular natural pyrotechnics during a great burst of volcanic activity.

The cone of Mount Gambier, the best known of the eight old volcanoes in the area, was formed in the last of the underground fireworks. Its summit now lies some 200 metres above the surrounding plain. Finely fragmented lava called ash are the main rocks that make up this classic cone, but a little dark volcanic basaltic rock is mixed with the finer material.

The beauty of the lake that fills the crater adds to the dramatic landform of the cone, although the superb blue of the water in summer changes to a less attractive grey in winter. A number of reasons have been advanced for the change in colour of Blue Lake. My own idea is that the fine silt that lies on the bottom is stirred up when winter cold chills the surface water and it then becomes more dense and flows downward. Winter storms also help keep the water moving, stopping washed-in silt from sinking so that the water remains murky.

Warm water is less dense than cold so with the arrival of spring and summer the waters on the surface remain as a top layer. The silt settles and the water looks brilliantly blue, a feature of any pool

Above:
The Blue Lake at Mt Gambier only remains a brilliant blue during the summer months, and changes to a less attractive grey during winter.

Left:
The Sturt Pea is South Australia's floral emblem.

where only the finest of particles remain suspended.

The colour is similar to the waters around Broome and Thursday Island where the sea is stirred by mammoth tides and the fine white silt reflects only the shorter blue waves of the sunlight spectrum.

A small part of the water filling Blue Lake comes from rain, but most is from an underground supply. The 6,000 square kilometre plain on which Mount Gambier stands is made of limestone, rock which allows water to sink through it. The rain falling in this area travels down until it reaches a layer of clay where it is held in an extensive underground pool.

Geologists call this the Gambier limestone aquifer. Beneath the clay layer, however, lies sand and gravel (called the Knight Sands aquifer) also excellent for holding water. Recent studies have shown that the Gambier aquifer has a plughole some 30 kilometres north of Mount Gambier and water flows from the top layer to fill the Knight aquifer.

In 1841 the water reached its lowest

level and since then has varied by as much as 8 metres. Indeed, with the clearing of the surrounding plain of forest, the general water table rose and so did the level of the lake. By 1910 it was at its highest recorded level, but today, due to its use as the city's water supply, it has dropped close to the level it was at in 1841.

The vent in the centre of the volcanic cone through which molten lava once poured, now forms a hole which penetrates deep into the earth, cutting through to the lower Knight aquifer. About 80 per cent of the lake's water appears to come from this lowest underground pool. This is fortunate as it means surface pollution, which might destroy the quality of the water near the top, does not affect most of the supply. It seems unlikely that the water of Blue Lake will lose its purity of colour or its quality.

PICCANINNIE PONDS

The limestone plains that surround Mount Gambier collect a vast amount of water from winter rains and when this has penetrated into the two aquifers already described, it runs slowly towards the sea.

Some, however, break through to the surface creating ponds, swamps and lakes. The best known of these, Piccaninnie Ponds, has given its name to a conservation park in the area.

A number of freshwater pools in the park run for about 3 kilometres parallel with the coastline and behind the sand dunes fronting the sea. Their underground caverns attract adventurous visitors. One of the deepest has been explored to a depth of 67 metres and more passageways go even further.

The bottoms are lined with silt so any disturbance can cloud the normally clear water and divers have died, unable to see their way back to the surface before exhausting their air supply. The National Parks and Wildlife Service now has strict guidelines to protect divers and they are warned of the dangers of the ponds.

The deep ponds are the main attraction here but the plants and animals are also of interest. Eels, long-necked swamp tortoises, freshwater crustaceans, pond snails, and a variety of fish live in the water, and there are also a number of rare plant species.

This intricate web of underwater caverns fed from freshwater springs will keep its quality only if the management of the whole of the Gambier Plains is

carefully planned. The preservation of the quality of a landscape is not a simple matter, and major changes to one area must be carefully considered. The beauty of Blue Lake and the Piccaninnie Ponds is too important to be lost through lack of conservation planning.

DALHOUSIE SPRINGS

In *King Solomon's Mines* the gallant party near death in the desert were saved by finding a pool of water in an unusual place, on top of a hill. Such mound springs are common in Australia as well as in other parts of the world.

They are artesian bores where water taken in thousands of kilometres away in the aquifers of the Great Dividing Range reaches the surface through a natural break in the rocks.

The Great Artesian Basin straddles most of western Queensland and spills over to northern New South Wales, the southeast corner of the Northern Territory and the northeast corner of South Australia. The main intake beds of the whole system are in the Queensland ranges.

The rocks of this vast basin contain evidence of a huge inward-draining lake system that appeared millions of years ago in Jurassic times. The sands laid down in that ancient lake changed down the ages to sandstones and today are the aquifers that hold artesian water.

Below and above these sandstones are mudstones and shales that act as an impervious layer: it is like a giant rock sandwich with the water-bearing beds being the filling.

A natural break in the overlying impervious rocks has created at Dalhousie a very large outlet of water from the basin. These springs are believed to be the largest active ones in Australia, but they are only one of many concentrations found in the area of the Great Artesian Basin. Others occur at Cunnamulla, Hughenden, and Cloncurry in Queensland, and at White Cliffs and near Bourke in New South Wales. South Australia has an arc of springs stretching from Lake Frome to Dalhousie.

The water, charged with a number of minerals dissolved out of underground rocks, comes to the surface and it is then that evaporation, over thousands of years, builds a small hillock. Recent drilling has shown also that at least some of the mounds are made of clay and sand which has been brought to the surface from the sediments of the Great Artesian Basin.

Top and above:
The Great Artesian Basin of Central Australia has been tapped by artesian bores to supply water for stock. Long before the white man arrived, however, natural breaks in the Basin which allowed water to come to the surface created ponds in a number of places from Queensland, through New South Wales to northern South Australia.

Dalhousie Springs are one of the most active of such natural artesian outlets. The outpouring water brought up material that created mounds. Some of the lakes contain freshwater fish and are also used for swimming.

The water pouring out of the top often creates considerable pools at the base. Coming from deep in the earth it reaches the surface near boiling and remains comfortably warm in the larger pools. One pool in the group at Dalhousie Springs is 400 metres long and has become a popular oasis in a forbidding desert.

The wildlife in mound springs, both in the water and in the vegetation on the slopes, has produced many surprises including species new to science. The most diverse freshwater fish on our continent thrive in these desert pools while reed beds, paperbarks, samphires and other water-loving plants grow vigorously around the springs and swamps.

Unfortunately, since their discovery the flow of water from many of these mound springs is decreasing, often because of other bores drilled nearby to provide water for stock. Grazing animals, ranging from sheep and cattle to rabbits, have damaged the plantlife.

The destruction of the mound springs will result not only in the disappearance of interesting plants and animals but also in a historical loss, particularly in terms of our Aboriginal prehistory, as around their bases lie the middens discarded during thousands of years of occupation. Such 'rubbish heaps' are scientific 'treasure houses' for an archaeologist.

MURRAY CLIFFS AT NILDOTTIE

The Murray-Darling system has played an important part in both Aboriginal and white history and had an impact on all the eastern mainland states. Early in this century an old Aboriginal said that when he was a young man, 'So many blackfellows lived along the river that no grass grew.'

The Murray-Darling system is the fourth longest river group in the world and in geological terms its history is ancient. (This is discussed in the Victorian section.) In South Australia the river takes a most unusual course, flowing west, then turning abruptly south.

Some geologists suggest it once had an outlet to the west in the Spencer Gulf; the right-angle change in direction certainly appears to be due to a fault-scarp blocking its path to the easier passage provided by jointing in the rocks through which it flows.

Between Morgan and Mannum the river flows in a wide and deep gorge. Charles Sturt, the explorer, commented on the 'bold and perpendicular cliffs of different shades of yellow colour, varying from light hue to deep . . .' The cliffs reveal an even greater beauty to campers today when at sunrise they are seen glowing warmly in the low sun across the still surface of the waters.

Right:
The Murray River near Mannum is a haven for waterbirds such as these cormorants.

Top right and far right:
The Flinders Ranges are part of the great mountain arc which begins at Kangaroo Island, runs north past Adelaide as the Mt Lofty Ranges, then sweeps on and includes attractions like Wilpena Pound, the Gammon Ranges and Arkaroola.

Some 15 to 20 million years ago a Miocene sea invaded this area of South Australia as well as nearby Victoria and New South Wales. On the retreat of the oceans during uplift the present Murray River developed and cut into the limestone rock created from the sediments laid down in that ancient sea.

In these yellowish rocks the most casual observer will see fossils of many kinds. At Nildottie the commonest are many species of heart urchins, including some sand-dollars. There are also ancient lampshells, and molluscs such as scallops, cowries, helmets, volutes and oysters.

In areas away from Nildottie, sharks' teeth and fragments of whale bone have also been found as fossils in rocks of the same age.

Another invasion of the sea in Pliocene times formed a narrow estuary. Between

Mannum and Morgan beds of sandstone show the cross bedding often found in rocks laid down in shallow waters. These also have a base bed of fossil oysters, deposited there a few million years ago. Then came changes in sea levels due to the ice ages of the last two million years. The final retreat of the sea accelerated the Murray River flow so that it cut deeply into its bed and created the gorges seen today.

On the bank opposite the high cliffs are points of sand and silt. The gradual widening of the flood plain of the river provided rich agricultural land so important for the early white settlers.

A river winding in a wide valley is deepest where it undercuts a cliff. The river steamers of earlier times found these ideal places to anchor close in and load or unload cargo. In earlier times the

Aboriginals found the same cliffs with their overhangs equally good for campsites. Protected from the weather and with easy access to fishing and other freshwater products these spots were reached by foot or in the frail, simply built canoes they used to negotiate the more placid of the river waters.

One of these rock shelters provided what was described in *The Heritage of Australia* as 'the classic excavation in Australian prehistory'. Since the first 'dig' at Devon Downs in 1929 a number of other sites such as Nildottie and one near Walkers Flat have shown an Aboriginal occupation of the area for the last 5,000 years.

In their study of this occupation two leading anthropologists, H. Hale and N. B. Tindale, found what appeared to be three cultural phases as revealed in the methods of working the stone tools used in those far-off times. The excitement produced by this rich sequence stimulated an outburst of interest in Australian prehistory that has continued to the present day.

THE FLINDERS RANGES

I first saw the Flinders Ranges as a low line of blue hills on the horizon and was struck by the contrast to the never-ending plains of the Nullarbor. The approach from the saltbush flats of the eastern side

The Gammon Ranges of the Northern Flinders are mainly horizontal beds of sandstone. A huge wilderness park has been reserved in this range which adjoins the older rocks of the Mt Painter region and Arkaroola.

had the same impact on me.

About half of South Australia is only 50 metres above sea level and 80 per cent is less than 300 metres, so the nearly 1,200 metre high St Marys Peak in Wilpena Pound seems much more dramatic than it would appear in a more varied landscape.

The Flinders Ranges are part of a great arc of mountains that begins at Kangaroo Island, swings past Adelaide at the Mount Lofty Ranges, then runs north to take in Wilpena Pound, the Gammon Ranges and Arkaroola. Their story began about 400 million years ago with the raising into mountains of a sequence of ancient rocks.

As soon as this uplift occurred, the forces of erosion set to work to smooth the mountains back into plains. Down the years the original fault lines remained areas of weakness and earth movements up or down until the last great uplift produced the Flinders Ranges as we know them today. The vertical lines of movement along these faults explain the abruptness of the rise. Evidence of the old uplifted plain is shown by the uniformity of the heights of the hilltops.

These movements took place fairly recently in geological times—beginning about 50 million years ago, rising to a maximum some five million years ago and continuing with little change for several more million years.

The following places are only a few of the picturesque natural wonders of the Flinders.

Gammon Ranges
This rugged area in the northern Flinders Ranges some 60 kilometres east of Copley was preserved as a national park in 1970. No roads actually reach the boundary, a measure of the true wilderness nature of the park. The World Wilderness Congress at Cairns defined this new sort of reserve as 'a large tract of entirely natural country. It is a place where one stands with the senses entirely steeped in nature and where one feels free of the effects of modern technology'.

Many of the natural wonders described in this book fall into such a category. The government is increasing the 16,000 hectares of the present park so the Gammon Ranges could become one of

the most famous of Australian wilderness reserves.

The rocks of the ranges are mainly sandstone, once a plateau but moulded by erosion into rounded hills broken by deep gorges. On the eastern edge the mountains front Lake Frome, with the cliffs of Cleft Peak Basin making this one of the most rugged of all areas in the Flinders.

Arkaroola

In the Aboriginal Dreamtime, Arkaroo, the giant serpent living in Main Water Pound in the High Gammon Ranges, southwest of Arkaroola, slithered down to the plains to slake its thirst.

In enormous drafts it drank Lake Frome and Callabonna dry, and with its belly full, commenced a slow retreat . . .

As in all Dreamtime legends the features of the landscape were then created; caves where it slept for the night, valleys where its body dragged along the ground, waterholes where it paused.

Arkaroo reached the Yacki Waterhole where it sleeps to this day, at times, however, it turns and the noise of its moving rumbles through the hills.

Reg and Griselda Sprigg, owners of the Arkaroola Station, told me the story of the giant snake. They have turned their mountainous retreat into a kind of private 'national park'. Reg, a geologist, said the rumbles of Arkaroo were caused by the slipping of the earth along active fault lines fronting the Gammons.

He also told me of a kilometre-long dry stone wall about a metre high. This appears to be not the work of shepherds as local legend has it, but an Aboriginal depiction of Arkaroo. Perhaps stones were added over thousands of years to the sinuous line that follows the contour halfway up the hillslope.

Arkaroola is an interesting contrast to the relatively simple rocks of the Gammons that have few minerals. Here the intruding granites brought in many rich ores. The most famous, the uranium deposits of Mount Painter, being the ore of radium, a valuable mineral even in earlier days, once caused a minor rush.

The original discoveries were made by Sir Douglas Mawson, famous as an Antarctic explorer, but here in his home state of South Australia revered as a geologist. One of his students was young Reg Sprigg and one memorable day as they stood and looked at this beautiful countryside Mawson turned to Reg saying, 'Sprigg you must do something to protect all this'.

Reg has carried out his wish in the project which has made Arkaroola known to all those who love the outback of Australia.

This fascinating landscape is rich in minerals, yet never developed into economically important fields despite its early promise. It escaped massive change by man and remains a haven for the new breed of gem hunter. A list of the principal minerals reads like an Aladdin's Cave — gold, sapphires, oriental ruby and emerald, turquoise, precious felspar,

amethyst and jasper. There are more than fifty minerals, including ores of copper, iron and radioactive materials.

One of the outstanding scenic features is the Ridgetops Road, a four-wheel drive journey of adventure that includes Mount Painter and ends at the hot springs of Paralana. This track, a byproduct of earlier mineral exploration, allows tourists, geologists and naturalists access to one of the finest educational areas in the arid regions of the northern Flinders Ranges.

Wilpena Pound

The hideaway of Captain Starlight and the Marstons in Rolf Boldrewood's *Robbery Under Arms* brought the romance of 'pounds' to many Australians and a visit to the natural pound of Wilpena enhances this feeling.

This vast dimple in the sandstone rocks appears to have been caused by an earth movement folding the thick beds of rock into a saucer shape. The upturned edges of the depression forms peaks and the highest of them is St Marys at 1,170 metres.

The 35 kilometre round rim encloses 70 square kilometres of hollow, the only break being in the northeast corner where Wilpena Creek runs through the gap, past the tourist resort on its way to the 'sink' of Lake Frome.

The quartzites of which the Pound is made originated in a shallow sea formed some 600 million years ago in the Upper Precambrian when a vast area of subsidence (known as the Adelaide Geosyncline) allowed sand and other sediments to pour in. The sinking of the sea bed enabled enormous deposits to accumulate and in some parts of the Flinders Ranges these layers reach 16,000 metres in thickness. The original rocks of the base are now kilometres below the land surface.

Earth movements later raised the sandstones and changed them into the harder quartzites that were folded to form Wilpena Pound. It is particularly interesting that in the original quartzites at Ediacara and other places in the region are fossil remains of soft-bodied animals. Their discovery created world-wide interest, and South Australia came to be regarded as a scientific paradise and the most famous of all the states in terms of its geology.

Arguing from the fact that a great range of complex animals appeared suddenly in the Cambrian period, geologists were certain there must have been a long

Left:
Arkaroola is a place of fascinating rocks and gemstones. Mt Painter is one of the high points dominating the area.

Over (pp. 178–9):
The saucer shape of Wilpena Pound appears to have been caused by earth movement.

177

period when evolution produced simpler animals and plants. Sir Douglas Mawson thought the best chance of finding such remains was in the almost undisturbed Precambrian rocks of the Flinders Ranges.

Reg Sprigg walked the hills of the Flinders Ranges ever alert for evidence of fossils. One memorable day, as he turned over rock slabs at Ediacara, he saw the outline of what, to him, was obviously a jellyfish as large as the palm of his hand. It was the first of many fossils to be found in this particular layer, but what was obvious to Reg was not as obvious to his associates. Only gradually was his interpretation accepted, partly because of the enthusiasm of Russian geologists attending an international conference.

It was a stroke of the greatest geological luck that on that day, some 600 million years ago, an ancient sea stranded myriads of these simpler marine creatures and, instead of them withering in the hot sun and being blown away by the wind, a sudden flood preserved them with a cover of silt.

As the years passed more sand was deposited on this fragile layer until it became sandstone, then it was changed to even harder quartzite, and finally revealed to the young geologist walking along what was an ancient shoreline. As well as jellyfish the assemblage of fossils includes sea pens, worms and other forms. Now regarded as not only the most abundant but the oldest collection of marine fauna, the site of Ediacara has been declared a reserve.

THE BADLANDS OF ARCKARINGA

Oodnadatta was the romantic jumping-off place for much northern exploration in central Australia. Anyone travelling across the dry country of northern South Australia towards this town will be enthralled by the changing skyline. Table-topped hills are broken by dry valleys in a pale yellow to deep red desert landscape.

The Arckaringa Hills and their beauty are little known as the road is not a popular tourist route. Rough and stony, it passes through an area of saline soils whose crusty red surface is often covered with a pavement of stones which may be silcrete, ironstone, or the outcropping bedrock of the area. Fragments may be up to 15 centimetres in diameter. Scientists think the soils of this particular region are the last stages of an old drainage system pouring south into Spencers Gulf, although today Arckaringa Creek spills into Lake Eyre.

Rainfall is sparse but during a storm it may come in a deluge. On such barren plains the eroding power of waterborne pebbles scours new valleys, scratches smooth slopes back into jagged terrain and creates the kind of landscape called 'badlands' in the USA.

It proved bad for early travellers, although some cattle stations survived. Wild camels, descendants of the magnificent animals brought to Australia by Thomas Elder for desert exploration, including the Burke and Wills expedition, are at home in this frightening country.

Elder's camels were carefully selected and because of their genetic superiority their wild descendants are now finding favour in their traditional home. A small export trade has begun and they are being sold back to the Middle East!

Beltana Station, north of Port Augusta, was the main breeding station for the animals and Oodnadatta the railhead from where camels took over during the major explorations of the last century. Although the handlers were called 'Afghans' they came from what is now Pakistan.

The rerouting of the railway to Alice Springs has isolated Oodnadatta, but it may yet flourish as a centre for the Aboriginal population of the area. Tourism is another income-earner. Some adventurous groups are already abandoning the four-wheel drive in favour of camels in treks to explore the badlands of Arckaringa, Dalhousie Springs and the Simpson Desert.

LAKE EYRE

I am the first person on record to be shipwrecked twice in the waters of Lake Eyre, and as the lake appears from past history to fill completely only twice in every century this is one record that is likely to stand!

Most lakes in Australia, saltwater or fresh, seem unlikely places to become storm-tossed, but strong winds over the expanse of Lake Eyre can produce a surf that crashes on the sandy beaches. From the air you might well believe you are flying over the coast, rather than the driest part of mainland Australia.

The early explorers, misled by the fact that the rivers draining an area as large as about 1·3 million square kilometres of inland eastern Australia all flowed towards the centre of the continent, decided there must be an inland sea since in good seasons the rivers ran bankers into the desert.

The mystery of the disappearing water was solved by explorer John Eyre in 1840 when he found the lake named in his honour. Indeed, he discovered a great boomerang of lakes which lay around the northern end of the Flinders Ranges. Lake Frome was on the western end of the boomerang, Lake Callabonna on the eastern, with Lake Eyre as the keystone.

Instead of an inland sea he found the world's largest salt pan. There is an estimated 500 million tonnes of salt among the mineral deposits in the lake bed.

The filling of both north and south Lake Eyre in 1974 to 1977 was the greatest in recorded history, the water

Left:
The badlands of Arckaringa have been tamed by better roads so that the traveller moving north from Oodnadatta can enjoy the spectacle of eroded hills without the fears of the early settlers who named them. Many of the colours of the area came from concretions of ironstone such as this one.

181

covering 9,300 square kilometres—about six times the area of Port Phillip Bay or in the unit of water measure equalling the water area of Sydney Harbour, 170 'Syd-harbs'.

The northern lake, 145 kilometres long and 65 kilometres wide, was joined by a water channel to the smaller southern lake, the two totalling about 10,000 square kilometres, making Lake Eyre sixteenth in a list of the great lakes of the world.

Yet 40,000 years ago it was at least three times as large as it is at present. It is no surprise to learn that the Aboriginals who lived on its shores when the white settlers arrived had Dreamtime legends of it as a place of great forests. Then it was a land flowing with milk and honey in terms of wildlife along its shores, and the waters would have teemed with fish and attracted myriads of waterbirds. The Aboriginals have been in Australia at least 40,000 years, possibly longer, so they would have known the great Lake Eyre and all its natural resources well.

Even the greatest modern filling of the lake is a temporary affair as the average rainfall is about 125 millimetres and the monthly evaporation rate during summer is as much as 300 millimetres.

This explains why even when the lake fills there is no change in climate in the region, except perhaps a slight leavening of the dryness very close to the shoreline.

The persistent dream of settlers that if we could only fill this enormous depression with water, either fresh or salt, it would change the climate, has been shown to be absurd during the two fillings of this century. A study of present-day shorelines along the Nullarbor and the northwest of Western Australia shows immediately that deserts can occur next to oceans.

Lake Eyre and its surroundings are fascinating in terms of geology. The lake is at the centre of a vast dip basin that first appeared some 150 million years ago. Changes in the landscape since then have resulted in the present lake being about 17 metres below the sea level. This lowering of the land appears to be

Above and right:
As they evaporate the waters of Lake Eyre leave behind strange crystal shapes of rock salt and gypsum. These two common minerals are carried here by the rivers which drain into the lake. Erosion cuts low cliffs in such material as the floodwaters rush into the lake, sometimes breaking through sandhills on their path.

Far right:
Cooper Creek, one of the long rivers of inland Australia, is usually dry. In the heavy rainfall years it fills with water which finally reaches Lake Eyre. Here it is pouring into the lake.

continuing and fault lines, cracks along which the earth slipped in its subsidence, explain why mound springs are found on the western edge where the cracks tapped the Great Artesian Basin. Lines of cliffs make a pleasant break in the monotony of the scenery dominated by dunes and salt flats. Both mound springs and cliffs lie along straight lines, the lines of the earth slips.

What of the salt that covers the southern section of the lake? The sea has not invaded this great depression during the last 80 million years so the salt is not a marine remnant. A certain amount is blown inland on the onshore winds but not enough to explain the huge deposits.

The river system bringing water to the lake drains a land mass partly composed of ancient marine sediments, and it is from these rocks that the salt has been leached by rain and running water, becoming concentrated in the depression of Lake Eyre when the water finally evaporates. The hollow, which artist John Olsen graphically describes as being like the plughole of Australia, has become choked with a bung of salt.

Camping on the edge of this lake when it is filled is a thrilling experience. At sunset, when a blood-red sun sinks toward a horizon unbroken by any land and the sea is as still as a mirror, it is easy to believe the Aboriginal legends of the Dreamtime spirit snake Kuddimukra.

The South Australian geologist Dr Madigan described it as 'a djinn-like spirit which may appear in the form of a giant snake with the head of a kangaroo, likely to do much harm to the unwary traveller'. Camped in this wilderness he wrote, 'The myths seemed to put on reality on that first night in this dark and silent desolation'.

But today as more and more Australians are exploring these desert regions, they appreciate Lake Eyre as part of the totality of the country we call home. And the waters of this desert sea will go and come again, and go once more in the ever-repeating pattern of nature.

Tasmania

THE SOUTHWEST

'The finest walking country in the world', said Sir Edmund Hillary of southwest Tasmania, a wilderness of 800,000 hectares, (which is one-fifth of the island) that has been in conservation headlines for nearly twenty years.

It was renowned for treasures such as Lake Pedder, now buried under the waters of a hydro-electric scheme, a host of ranges, including Federation and the Western Arthurs, and a landscape sculpted by the great ice sheets that covered much of the central and western highlands in fairly recent times. Indeed the moraines, cirques, and other features of the ice sheets provide much of the dramatic scenery, including the 4,000 lakes.

There are many rivers spectacular for Australia in their torrential progress, the amount of water they carry, and the fact that they flow all year, rather than dwindle in dry times in the fashion so common among the rivers of the mainland.

The Gordon, Franklin, Davey and Huon Rivers became household words during the great conservation controversy when the proposed dam on the Franklin River polarised Australian opinion.

Human faces are smooth with babyhood and begin to wrinkle with maturity. A landscape is the opposite, youth being a time of wildness in the life of a river and the land through which it flows. Gorges, rapids and waterfalls are common and with maturity these wrinkles on the landscape are removed as the waters sweep to the sea carrying loads of sediment. The pace of the river slackens with age as it winds through rounded hills smoothed of most of their angularity.

So it is with the Gordon and other rivers. They flowed over the ancient rocks of the mountains where the tough, erosion-resistant quartzites remained while the softer schists were carved by the rushing waters to form narrow gorges.

It is not the water that does the eroding but the material it contains. Water-driven sand grains scrape at the river bed just as the wind-driven sand of the desert sculpts the rocks over which it blows. After storms large pebbles and even boulders become battering rams that shatter the rocks of the river bed whose fragments are then carried triumphantly away by the flood waters.

Because of the significant landforms, the archaeological value, and the wealth of wildlife that included 165 plant species found only in Tasmania, (twenty-nine of them found only in the southwest) both the state and federal governments

Left:
The Franklin near the Lyell Highway. This river became world famous during the conservation battle to save it and is now part of the Wild Rivers National Park.

Right:
The upper reaches of the Gordon River show some of the dramatic valleys which make this part of southwest Tasmania so important as a reserve.

Below:
Butlers Island in the Gordon River, now part of the southwest national park.

nominated the area for World Heritage listing.

They put together the three national parks, Cradle Mountain-Lake St Clair, the Franklin-Lower Gordon Wild River National Park, and the Southwest National Park, to make a new reserve of 770,000 hectares to be known as the Western Tasmania Wilderness National Parks and this nomination was accepted by the World Heritage Committee in December 1982.

THE SPLITS

The Aboriginals would have known the narrow gorges on the Gordon River through their tens of thousands of years of occupation of this mountainous island, but the first whites to explore them would have been 'piners'—those intrepid men who searched for the 'white gold' of huon pine.

This rugged stretch of the Gordon River came into wider knowledge officially as late as 1928. Conservationist Mike Emery wrote in *The Southwest—a Tasmanian Wilderness*, 'Abel, Sticht and Harrison . . . discovered them in 1928 in an epic trip up the river using a small punt (helped by an exceptionally dry summer) and named them The Splits'.

The First, Second, and Third Splits are named as though travelling upstream by boat, though most present-day accounts are written by canoeists and rafters travelling downstream with the water. Mike Emery described their dramatic nature as 'a series of narrow vertical cracks separated by small basins, through which the whole of the Gordon flows. One split is so narrow you have to hold your paddle parallel to the canoe . . . two dark, vertical, sculpted walls rising to between 100 and 200 feet; shiny, scalloped, patterned. Between them the water is quite still and deep . . .'.

In the early planning days of the Western Tasmania Wilderness Parks a wealth of cultural material lay unsuspected. Eight kilometres downstream from the First Splits a fallen tree turned up artefacts from a 300-year-old Aboriginal campsite. Then a search began for more sites and in 1977 a new cave was found on the Franklin some 10 kilometres from where it joins the Gordon River. It was first named Fraser Cave

after the prime minister who at the time said he was determined to preserve this southwestern heritage.

Kutikina Cave has about 100 square metres of floor with passages stretching 150 metres into the limestone rock. It was revealed as dazzlingly rich in Aboriginal artefacts. One cubic metre provided more than 80,000 stone flakes and tools and it is estimated that the whole cave contains some ten million objects.

More sites have been found since, one at least promising to be as important as Kutikina Cave. The 100 square kilometres of this karst region of the wild rivers almost certainly has hundreds of caves, making it one of the most important areas of use by ice-age people anywhere in the world. It has similarities to the famous caves of southern France, although the Aboriginals, instead of hunting deer, captured wallabies, wombats and echidnas.

Aboriginals moved south into this new country, along the exposed continental shelves, during the earth's last Ice Age, 23,000 years ago. Before that Tasmania was an island with sea levels much as they are today. When the Ice Age locked water into solid sheets, sea levels fell around the world and Tasmania became joined once more to the mainland.

A band of twenty or thirty people found Kutikina Cave an ideal home, providing shelter against the ice and snow, for 18,000 years ago glaciers were flowing down the Franklin Valley. Rainforests grew along their edges and here the people hunted. They travelled 40 kilometres to the northwest to the Darwin meteorite crater to get natural glass formed by the heat of the collision. These people of so long ago found nature's glass valuable enough to justify a long journey over rugged country.

About 14,000 years ago on the retreat of the glaciers the Kutikina Cave people were able to leave as food became plentiful and the surrounding country, freed from the sheets of ice, offered better hunting. The glaciers and ice sheets left behind the landforms that are a permanent reminder of the once most glaciated countryside in all Australia.

Describing southwest Tasmania the anthropologist Dr Josephine Flood wrote, 'The courage and skill of these Tasmanian Aborigines, braving the ice, snow and freezing cold to hunt wallabies, within

sight of glaciers, is eloquent testimony to the indomitable spirit of early humans'.

We can be proud of our early history. What a tragedy it would have been if this wealth of historical material and scientific information had been buried 50 metres deep under the waters of a dam, not vital to Tasmania's present needs! It would have been as though a unique library had been destroyed before scholars had time to read any of the books.

FRENCHMANS CAP

A perennial task for white explorers in Australia was to name the notable geographical features they discovered. It was easy to honour the person who provided the opportunity for the explorer to start his journey. Royalty was a popular choice, then governors, and finally the rich and powerful. The names used by the original Australians could be useful, but because the Tasmanian Aboriginals were a despised race few of their names for the landforms were retained.

The glistening white mountain that rears dramatically above the skyline about 200 kilometres from Hobart on the Lyell Highway resembles the cap once worn by the ordinary French worker. This 1,400 metre high Frenchmans Cap is part of the southern plateau, an extension of the central highlands. But it is unusual as, unlike the ever-present dolerite of the plateau surface, its resistant rocks are a white quartzite.

The surrounding countryside was moulded by glaciers during the last 50,000 years. Some 12,000 years ago the ice had gone from places such as Lake Vera at 560 metres, although it lingered in the higher cirques. In the area of the Cap, eight cirques and their valley glaciers have been identified. These hollows in the mountain side, produced by the plucking and weathering of the ice, finally joined to make the striking-looking Frenchmans Cap.

On the southeastern face a cliff soars 300 metres up while the northwest slope is more rounded, and this combination of

Right:
Mt Anne from Mt Eliza. This high point is part of the systems that led Sir Edmund Hillary to call Tasmania 'the best walking country in the world'.

rock faces has made the peak a mecca for many rock climbers.

The walking track from the highway leads across sodden plains in most seasons. It is said that from highway to summit can be traversed in nine hours, but Tasmania's changing weather makes all such estimates uncertain.

A variety of plants and animals typical of the forest and plain areas of the southwest live in the park named after the peak. The wildlife history of the area has been studied in some detail and in *The Southwest Book* what happened after the glaciers retreated is traced. Much of the evidence comes from pollen sediments in Lake Vera and shows that while the glaciers flowed to the sea from the slopes of mountains such as the Franklands, the Arthurs, and Mount Anne, the locking up of so much water in ice dropped sea levels more than 100 metres. This meant that the sea cliffs of today's west coast were

then a long way from the sea.

Just before the last retreat of the glaciers much of the southwest was a treeless tundra, familiar in the present northern hemisphere but missing in Australia. As the conditions improved for plants, Antarctic beech forests clothed the slopes of the Cap and treeferns became common. There is also strong evidence that a dramatic change some 5,000 years ago was probably caused by fires on the lowlands spreading inland. Firing of the forest was one of the major causes of change produced by Aboriginal occupation everywhere in Australia.

Fire caused the rainforests to retreat and eucalypt invaders as well as other plants to take over. Today when fire is excluded by human intervention from many areas, we can sometimes see the advance of the rainforests once more in particular areas, both in Tasmania and on the mainland.

It is this study of the present and the past that makes reserves such as Frenchmans Cap National Park important. Once a lake sediment is drowned by a dam, then its evidence is lost forever. From a patient study of our past we may get timely warning for our future. So national parks are not only places for recreation—they are also like books in a scientific library whose text we are only now beginning to be able to read.

CRADLE MOUNTAIN— LAKE ST CLAIR

For a bushwalker in wild country certain memories remain sharply etched. One such memory is the first sight of the Weindorfer Chalet on the edge of Cradle Mountain with red-necked wallabies grazing peacefully on the clearing in front of the building.

On the top of the nearby mountain on 4 January in 1910 Gustav Weindorfer exclaimed, 'This must be a national park for the people for all time. It is magnificent, and people must know about it and enjoy it'.

Weindorfer was not a man of words alone. He and his wife Kate laboured to achieve their dream, building a chalet which they named Waldheim or 'forest home', constructed from the King Billy pine trees growing nearby. Weindorfer died with part of his dream fulfilled, but today it is a complete reality.

The old chalet has been restored and in the nearby cabins brushtail possums come to the table to share a visitor's meal in the evening.

This park enshrines the philosophy of the American writer Thoreau, who, being very different from most people of the 19th century, wrote 'In wildness is the preservation of the world'.

Left:
Crater Lake on the Overland Track. This walk through the Cradle Mountain–Lake St Clair National Park is the most famous of all bushwalking trails in Australia.

Above:
A plant whose botanical name is *Aciphylla Procumbens* is found growing on the summit at Lake St Clair.

189

Above right:
Acropolis du Cane Range in the Lake St Clair National Park.

Right below:
Central Highlands, Cradle Mountain.

Far right:
Mossy Creek rainforest in the Lake St Clair National Park.

Over (pp. 192–3):
Cradle Mountain was so named because the dolerite cliffs have been worn by glacial action into the shape of a baby's cradle.

The Overland Track—83 kilometres of enthralling country, much of it above the 1,200 metre level—soon made the park famous among walkers. The track is well defined, even in high summer, but a sudden blizzard may bring disaster to the ill-prepared. Today walkers discuss the problem with the national park ranger before they leave to avoid the tragedies that have occurred in the past.

Beginning at Waldheim the first height to be scaled is that of Cradle Mountain, so named because the dolerite cliffs have been worn by glacial action into the shape of a baby's cradle. Nestling below are placid lakes lined with pines and moorland.

During the last few million years an ice sheet covered this area and the sheer walls of Cradle Mountain are due to the plucking action of the ice. In such places the water freezes and in so doing expands and breaks the rock surface. Over long periods of time this hollows out the mountain to form what is called a cirque. As a glacier moves forward it also gouges out the valley floor and walls. As a result the back wall of dolerite of Cradle Mountain rises some 600 metres above the valley floor. Similar landforms can be found at Barn Bluff and at the head of Pine Valley.

Tasmania as a whole is made of two broad structural rock types. The oldest are folded rocks showing invasions by granite and these form the basement in many places. Overlying them are sediments of several kinds that have been invaded by volcanic rocks, molten dolerites and basalts.

Western Tasmania has the best development of the basement rocks, while eastern and central Tasmania have the greatest exposures of the cover rocks. Block faulting and the resistance of the dolerites has created the striking plateaus and scarps of a dramatic landscape known locally as The Tiers. It is these dolerites that dominate the Cradle Mountain section of the park.

The central section is the Pelion Region, named after a mountain in Greece, the home of the centaurs. At times a weary walker may have wished for the four legs of a centaur as an aid to scaling these mountains.

It would be tiring to list all the twenty-five major peaks which rise in this region, with Mount Ossa of 1,617 metres being Tasmania's highest. The geology is complex, basically Precambrian granites and schists overlain by sediments of several kinds, including sandstones and mudstones with intrusions of black dolerites which in places form horizontal sills 300 metres thick. These harder volcanic rocks often create the most dramatic shapes in a country which has been moulded by the ice sheets.

Mount Pelion East, which stands on the horizon, has survived as an erosion remnant as the dolerite columns which form it are more resistant than the sandstone rocks on which they lie.

At the southern end of the park is Lake St Clair, thought to have been created at the base of a mountain when two glaciers came together to gouge out a deep hollow. After the ice went it filled with water. The present lake is more than 200 metres deep, 13 kilometres long and about 1·5 kilometres wide.

It was first reported by surveyor W. S. Sharland, the grandfather of one of Tasmania's best-known naturalists, Michael Sharland.

In country as rugged as this there are always a number of falls. The most famous here is D'Alton Falls near the Du Cane hut, a triplet waterfall that plunges for some 58 metres.

In this large park the wildlife affords a good cross-section of all that may still be found in Tasmania. Rainforests merge into wet forests, moorlands into button-grass plains. Deciduous beech splash the forests with colour in autumn while cushion plants are a feature of the high country.

The mammals include wallabies of several kinds, native and tiger quolls, the Tasmanian devil, and even possibly that Holy Grail of all naturalists, the Tasmanian tiger.

Birdlife is prolific and the mountain streams contain one of the world's largest freshwater crayfish, as well as a scientifically interesting primitive straight-backed shrimp.

Now that the Western Tasmania Wilderness National Parks (which includes the old Lake St Clair-Cradle Mountain park) has become a reality, the entire area offers a wilderness experience equalling anything elsewhere in the world.

THE NUT

Dominating the northwest town of Stanley is a dark, steep-sided mass of rock. The last of an ancient volcano, it rises some 120 metres from the sea and is fittingly named The Nut.

Between 40 and 15 million years ago huge masses of basalt poured from the interior of the earth over the land. As the fiery mountains calmed into a quiescent old age the lava solidified in their throats forming plugs of dark erosion-resistant basalt.

Over 200 such volcanic vents have been found, usually in the form showed by The Nut.

TASMAN PENINSULA—EAGLEHAWK NECK

Governor Arthur, discovering a land mass cut off almost entirely from the rest of Tasmania, except for a neck narrowed to 20 metres at its thinnest point, had a ready-made, easily guarded prison, and so the convict settlement of Port Arthur was

Left and below right:
Eaglehawk Neck is the strip of land that links the Peninsula with the rest of Tasmania. Eaglehawk is the old name for the wedgetail eagle.

Below left:
A blowhole at Eaglehawk Neck.

Left:
A basalt residual plug which shows The Nut in the background.

Above left:
Dolerite columns at Cape Hauy on the Tasmanian Peninsula. Dolerite is a volcanic rock that shrinks on cooling to form straight-sided pillars.

Below left:
Cape Hauy, Tasman Peninsula.

Below right:
The Candlestick, Cape Hauy, Tasman Peninsula.

established on Tasman Peninsula. Inspiration for the name Eaglehawk Neck possibly came from the presence of a wedgetail eagle flying overhead at the time.

Our wedgetail eagle is a far more magnificent species than the golden eagle of Great Britain, yet the early settlers tacked the diminutive 'hawk' on to its name, using two words to do the work of one.

Tasman Peninsula is visited by more tourists than any other place in the state. Its coast is about 240 kilometres round and shows the results of its flooding by a rising sea as the ice age waned. The sea drowned many areas, creating islands and near-islands such as this peninsula, re-forming Bass Strait, and cutting Tasmania off from the mainland once more.

Today most of the peninsula's coast, except the western side, is dominated by cliffs often rising to 200 metres, with ridges covered with forests rising to more than double that height. On the sea edge the cliffs have been cut into a series of blowholes, stacks, arches and caves, many of which have become major tourist attractions. Such high points offer spectacular coastal scenery.

TESSELLATED PAVEMENT

Slightly to the north of Eaglehawk Neck a tiny reserve protects an extraordinary rockform that looks like a man-made platform covered with paving stones.

A close inspection reveals that the rocks are mudstone or siltstone varying in composition as the original mud contained a proportion of sand.

Their even pattern is due to jointing. Joints are important in producing landforms everywhere in the world, so their study is worthwhile. They are fractures in rocks where there is no evidence that the two sides of the break have actually moved. If the earth in the region moves than it is called a fault, but at times it is hard to decide when a joint merges with a fault or vice versa.

Joints can be produced by far-off earth movements causing cracking or they can be due to the cooling of a molten rock. They also occur in sediments that are compressed or dried out as they consolidate. This explains their formation at the Tessellated Pavement.

As joints are also lines of weakness where wind, rain and water can penetrate and weather away even the hardest of rock, their importance in the shaping of the land cannot be overestimated.

At this pavement on the Tasmanian east coast powerful sea waves have smoothed and polished the surface and etched out the joint lines making their resemblance to a man-made pavement even more striking.

TASMAN ARCH

A coastline hammered by the waves suffers in many ways. The water pressure on impact helps erode the cliffs, particularly in the Tasman Peninsula where the sedimentary mudstones are horizontally bedded and broken by joints running at right angles. Both air and water under pressure can penetrate along such lines of weakness. When rocks break along these joint lines, the waves use the fragments of sand and shingle to pound the rest of the rock face and retreating water carries the fragments out to sea.

The first stage is usually for a cave to develop along the joints. As the hollow lengthens the water gradually breaks through cracks in the roof and a blowhole is formed. Water driven by waves carries with it air compressed by the movement that bursts out in spectacular fashion, particularly during storms.

Erosion continues to the stage where the rear of the cave finally collapses, leaving the more resistant parts as an arch—as in this famous landform.

Waves push along the main horizontal

Right:
Tasman Arch near Eaglehawk Neck, a dramatic landform created by the erosion of the sea.

Far right:
The Tessellated Pavement near Eaglehawk Neck. The geometrical pattern formed as the sand and mud changed to solid rock.

joints, work sideways along another line of joints (at right angles as well as vertically towards the surface) and finally bring the whole structure tumbling to make a landform such as the Devils Coachhouse where the rushing waters create an awe-inspiring cauldron in the deep cleft in the rocks.

Further south there is an earlier example of erosion called Remarkable Cave. Here a long tunnel through the cliffs dries out at low tide to give an eerie access to the sea. Backed by coastal heathlands, a disappearing habitat in most parts of Australia, this cave is today part of a small, yet scientifically important reserve.

CAPE PILLAR

The dolerite intrusions that dominate so many of Tasmania's scenic features are injected as molten material, but often cool into formations called 'organ pipes'. The reason for this kind of structure is explained in detail in the section on the Organ Pipes National Park in Victoria (p. 1).

The organ pipe cliffs of Cape Pillar rise vertically from the sea for about 300 metres. Waves pound ceaselessly at their base and fragments tumble into the sea creating rock platforms that offer a safe refuge for colonies of fur seals. These animals are gradually recovering their numbers after the ruthless hunting of the early days of white settlement.

The Cape Pillar Reserve of some 3,000 hectares protects this spectacular landform—the most southeasterly projection of the Tasman Peninsula—as well as the heaths of the summit from where there are splendid views of Tasman Island and Cape Raoul.

EXIT CAVE

In Tasmania the most spectacular cave complexes are at Mole Creek, Gunns Plains and Hastings. Since those better-known caves were discovered and publicised two more have become famous; they are Fraser Cave (or Kutikina), once threatened with drowning by the Franklin Dam, and Exit Cave near Ida Bay, 10 kilometres from the Lune River.

Exit Cave is part of the longest cave system (about 16 kilometres) in Australia, with a shaft some 200 metres deep leading to the cave from a ridge in thick bush country. Because of its size it contains a wide variety of cave animals, including colonies of glow worms. The Australian Heritage Register states 'Exit Cave is of world class and contains intrinsically valuable cave fauna . . .'

The limestones of this area have led to

Right:
Russells Falls, Mt Field National Park.

Above:
'Mother and Child', Hastings Cave.

Left:
Entrance to King Solomon's Throne Room, King Solomon's Caves, Mole Creek.

Far left:
Shawls coloured with iron minerals glow in the light in Hastings Cave.

Over (pp. 204–5):
The painted cliffs at Hopground Beach on Maria Island. This island is a nature reserve where some of Tasmania's rarer animals have been released.

the development of the magnificent caves found here. When water sinks underground, it can continue to erode if it is penetrating rocks that can be dissolved either by water itself, or by water containing carbonic acid. This acid is formed when carbon dioxide in the air or in humus, dissolves to form a natural soda water. Soda water is a weak acid but is capable of reacting chemically with lime to form a soluble material.

Should this lime-charged water become exposed to fresh air, the gas bubbles away and the lime is redeposited. So nature destroys and builds in a continuing cycle.

At the water table, where the rocks are saturated, such acid in the groundwater can dissolve caverns in the limestone. It may make sizeable channels and in such areas rivers often disappear underground, only to reappear many kilometres away. Mystery Creek is a river whose underground travels are part of the Exit Cave system.

Having eaten out the limestone to form caverns where the water table falls, the same water may begin to fill the hollows with a fascinating series of stalactites from the roof, or stalagmites from the floor. At times these may join to form a pillar. Shawls of material form along cracks and there are many other shapes, some of whose origins are a mystery. Other chemicals, particularly iron minerals, may stain shawl and other formations, resulting in patterns of great beauty.

THE TALLEST HARDWOOD TREE IN THE WORLD

Overpowering in its visual impact is a grove of mountain ash in the Styx Valley in Tasmania that holds the world's tallest hardwood and eleven other trees over 90 metres high. It would be a tragedy if this grove of giants were ever destroyed.

This mountain ash of 98·75 metres is

the world's tallest flowering plant as well as the tallest hardwood. North America can boast the world's tallest tree, a Californian redwood at 112·11 metres, but this tree is a softwood. Deep in the forests of mountain ash that cover much of Tasmania and parts of Victoria there may still be a tree even taller than the mountain ash of nearly 99 metres, and perhaps one that overtops the Californian redwood. The Cornthwaite tree, called after the surveyor who measured it, was said to be 114·3 metres tall, but as his field notes cannot be found the figure is in dispute. Yet trees of 103 metres were recorded in the last century, and a tree that fell after the disastrous 1939 fires was measured at 103 metres, with a possible extra 3 metres broken off in the fall.

Mountain ash is a smooth, bluish-grey tree, whose remnants of bark hang in ribbons, particularly near the base. It grows best in well-drained moist soils, especially in mountain gullies, which explains the name, 'mountain ash'. In southern Tasmania it is better known as the swamp gum and northerners call it the stringybark. In the furniture trade it is called Tasmanian oak and on the mainland, mountain ash. The scientific name *regnans* is a tribute to the regal nature of this forest giant.

It is one of the most important timber trees we have and the beauty of its pale colour, its lightness in weight, and the ease of working it in furniture and joinery all make it eagerly sought after. The rising use of hardwoods for papermaking has made the mountain ash the most important tree in the wood pulp industry.

World winner or not as the tallest tree, the magic of a mountain ash forest can never be defeated in terms of sheer beauty.

Conservation

The idea of nature being worth preserving is a modern one. Even the word 'landscape' is new, coming into the English language about the year 1600 and then used mainly by painters.

Like all new ideas this one had its roots in various countries. The nature poets of England helped shape the thoughts of many Americans and in that country the first major steps were taken to give the preservation of nature a massive legal framework.

In 1864 the sequoias of the Yosemite Valley in California were converted into timber with little thought being given to their grandeur. Concerned citizens managed to save a fragment of the stands for the enjoyment of future generations.

In 1872 there was a great leap forward. A walking party in the Yellowstone region were so impressed by its natural beauty that they welcomed the suggestion of one of the group that this unspoiled landscape should not be given away in land and timber concessions but should become the heritage of all Americans for all time. So was born the world's first truly national park.

Seven years later in New South Wales the second 'national' park was created near Sydney. A state reserve, it is not national in the legal sense, (Uluru and Kakadu were our first national parks.) Yet in the sense that such reserves are relatively large areas set aside because of their features of unspoiled natural landscape and associated wildlife, permanently dedicated for public enjoyment, education and inspiration and protected from all interference except that needed for essential management, then most of our state reserves deserve to be called National Parks.

We have come a long way, but we still have a long way to go before Australia has a satisfactory national park system. Only about 4 per cent of the variety of our landscapes and wildlife is protected as part of our permanent national heritage. It is internationally accepted that a minimum for such dedication is 5 per cent of a nation's area. Not just any 5 per cent, but a carefully selected sampling of diversity.

Just as the land needs conserving, so too does the sea. We have made a wonderful move forward in the declaration of the Great Barrier Reef as a new kind of marine regional park. Huge sections are preserved as marine national parks, in the true sense of the word. Yet such marine reserves are almost entirely missing in the rest of Australia.

A relatively new concept of 'wilderness park' has still to gain acceptance in Australia. These were first given legislative existence in the United States in 1964 when a Wilderness Act was passed. Wilderness is a more sophisticated type of national park where vast tracts show no obvious impact by man.

They can be defined as a special kind of national park: large enough to survive unchanged for the foreseeable future and where a visitor can experience a world unchanged by man. Visitors must take in a minimum of material aids and leave no trace of their stay.

Roads, bridges, vehicles and fire trails are not available in true wilderness. The visitor travels on foot, or in some special areas by horse.

It is interesting to see how the states compare in terms of the percentage of their total area reserved for nature conservation. The Australian Capital Territory heads the list with 25·63 per cent, Tasmania has 14·08 per cent, Western Australia 5·56 per cent, Victoria 4·79 per cent, South Australia 4·53 per cent, New South Wales 3·77 per cent, Queensland 1·94 per cent and the Northern Territory 0·92 per cent.

One field still awaits legislative protection, areas sometimes called 'regional parks' (in Great Britain known as 'national' parks, which is an incorrect use of the term). Regional parks are declared over landscapes where natural features and the works of man have combined to make a harmonious whole.

Such beauty is fragile and unsympathetic developments may ruin what generations of human endeavour has created. Planning controls are imposed to protect the regional park. A poorly sited factory, a quarry, a winding road turned into a super highway, out-of-character buildings or advertising signs could destroy the tranquillity of such places.

Every state in Australia has regions where farmland, treescapes and natural landforms together make a particularly agreeable scene. There is a move among conservationists to have the National Trust and the Australian Heritage Commission classify such regional landscapes.

This will be the first step in developing public interest so that in time the various governments concerned will legislate to protect them. Most of the power to conserve our natural beauty rests with state governments, although the formation of the Australian Heritage Commission in 1975 brought federal involvement on a major scale.

During the next six years the Commissioners, of which I was one, laboured to list all 'the things we want to keep' whether they were a farmer's simple cottage, a historic building, a significant tree, the sweep of an alpine area or a marine wonderland. The result was brought to public notice in a kind of domesday book, the massive *The Heritage of Australia*, a description of the 6,600 places already on the Register.

Another giant move forward came from the Convention for the Protection of the World Cultural and Natural Landscape, adopted by the General Conference of UNESCO in 1972 and usually called the World Heritage List.

Australia not only accepted this Convention as part of its international obligations but also had five places on the Australian Heritage Register nominated for world recognition. These were Kakadu National Park in the Northern Territory, the Great Barrier Reef Marine Park, Lord Howe Island, Lake Mungo in New South Wales and the Southwest Wilderness of Tasmania—all five aptly described as natural 'crown jewels'.

The listing of the Southwest Wilderness created conservation history. The Tasmanian Government had agreed to the nomination but there was a political change and the new government tried to withdraw it. When this failed, it decided to go ahead with a development which would have destroyed a vital part of the wilderness—the damming of the last of the great wild rivers of Tasmania.

Whether the Federal Government should, indeed whether they could, intervene, became a hotly contested question. A change of government at

The new Lake Pedder from Mt Eliza. The old Lake Pedder was a gem of exquisite beauty and although all such man-made water reservoirs have their attractions most conservationists mourn the loss of the old lake.

Federal level brought into power a party determined to honour Australia's obligations under the terms of the World Heritage Convention.

After a challenge as to the validity of the newly passed World Heritage Conservation Properties Act, the High Court decided in favour of the Commonwealth and work on the dam stopped.

The seed sown long ago in 1879 has grown to sturdy proportions. The last twenty years have seen a steady growth in public concern about the quality of our environment. First concentrated on national parks, it has spilled over into urban environments.

Australia led the world in the creation of the Green Ban, when trade unionists acted to preserve urban bushland as well as areas of historic buildings.

Every political party, both state and federal, must now take account of the growing involvement of voters in the environment. It seems unlikely that any party careless of the quality of life, either in the cities or in the country, will gain power in the years to come.

The conservation lobby is backed by some 400,000 (and increasing) adult members of natural history and conservation societies.

The future of the natural areas described in this book seems safe, but if the price of liberty is eternal vigilance, then the same is true of the quality of our environment.

Thoreau wrote, 'I went to the woods because I wished to live deliberately, to front only the essential facts of life, and see if I could not learn what it had to teach, and not, when I came to die, discover that I had not lived'.

From this experience came his book *Walden*. All of us need our own Walden. It need not be the beautiful woods of Thoreau's Concord in the United States; it can be an Australian forest, a lonely dune, a patch of urban bushland or a wild mountain place where few humans venture.

For the 'Waldens' we possess today we are indebted to the conservationists of previous generations. It is our task to protect what we still have, and to increase the amount of wildness to keep pace with our growing population. We did not inherit this earth from our parents, we are only trustees of it for our children.

Acknowledgements

The author, Vincent Serventy, would like to give special thanks to photographer, Gunther Deichmann, who took the majority of photographs in this book; and also for his invaluable assistance as picture editor.

The author and publisher would like to thank the following for permission to use their photographs in this book:

Jocelyn Burt (pp. 1–5; pp. 10–12 (top); p. 13 (above); p. 16; p. 71 (bottom); pp. 80–3; pp. 124–5; p. 133 (bottom two); p. 152; p. 160; p. 170; pp. 176–7; p. 183; p. 188; p. 190 (right below); pp. 200–1; pp. 204–5).

Neville Coleman (pp. 30–5).

Gunther Deichmann (p. viii; pp. x–xi; pp. 22–3; p. 23 (top); pp. 24–5; p. 27 (above); pp. 28–9; pp. 36–8; pp. 40–1; pp. 43–4; p. 48; p. 52 (bottom); pp. 53–71; pp. 75–7; pp. 84–121; p. 135; p. 137; pp. 138–42; pp. 144–51; pp. 154–5; pp. 158–9; pp. 161–6; p. 169; pp. 171–5; p. 180).

R. V. Eussen (pp. 72–3).

Ray Joyce (p. 20).

Lansdowne Library (pp. 6–9; p. 13 (left and top); pp. 14–15; p. 71 (below right); p. 122; pp. 126–8; pp. 132–3; p. 143; p. 153; p. 157; p. 182).

Reg Morrison (p. 12 (bottom); p. 21; p. 23; p. 26; p. 27 (above left); p. 39; p. 42; p. 45; pp. 78–80; p. 111 (right); pp. 129–31; p. 136; p. 167; pp. 178–9; pp. 184–7; p. 189; p. 190 (above right); pp. 191–9; pp. 202–3; pp. 208–9).

Rigby Publishers' Library (p. 138 (above); p. 168).

Ron & Valerie Taylor (pp. 50–1; p. 52 (top and middle)).

Index